Gervase Wheeler

A Driftless Connecticut Series Book

This book is a 2011 selection in the DRIFTLESS CONNECTICUT SERIES, *for an outstanding book in any field on a Connecticut topic or written by a Connecticut author.*

Gervase Wheeler

A BRITISH ARCHITECT IN AMERICA
1847–1860

Renée E. Tribert and James F. O'Gorman

WESLEYAN UNIVERSITY PRESS *Middletown, Connecticut*

Frontispiece:
Gervase Wheeler, Henry Hill Boody House, Brunswick, Maine, 1848–49. The projecting entrance porch is later. (O'Gorman photo, 2008)

An exhaustive effort has been made to locate the rights holder for the photograph of the Edward Bartlett residence (Figure 13) and to clear reprint permission. If the required acknowledgments have been omitted, or any rights overlooked, it is unintentional and understanding is requested.

Wesleyan University Press gratefully acknowledges the assistance of Furthermore: a program of the J. M. Kaplan Fund.

Wesleyan University Press
Middletown CT 06459
www.wesleyan.edu/wespress
© 2012 Renée E. Tribert and James F. O'Gorman
All rights reserved
Manufactured in the United States of America
Typeset in Miller, Clarendon and Didot types

The Driftless Connecticut Series is funded by the Beatrice Fox Auerbach Foundation Fund at the Hartford Foundation for Public Giving.

Wesleyan University Press is a member of the Green Press Initiative. The paper used in this book meets their minimum requirement for recycled paper.

Library of Congress
Cataloging-in-Publication Data
Tribert, Renee.
Gervase Wheeler: a British architect in America, 1847–1860 / Renée Tribert and James F. O'Gorman. — 1st ed.
  p. cm. — (Garnet)
Includes bibliographical references and index.
ISBN 978-0-8195-7145-8 (cloth: alk. paper) —
ISBN 978-0-8195-7146-5 (ebook)
1. Wheeler, Gervase — Criticism and interpretation. 2. Architecture — United States — History — 19th century. 3. Architects — Great Britain — Biography. I. Wheeler, Gervase. II. O'Gorman, James F. III. Title.
NA997.W463T75   2011
720.92 — dc23   2011035007
[B]

5 4 3 2 1

*To the memory of
Monica and Claude Tribert,
who always believed.*
—Renée E. Tribert

*and

Kell and "Birthel," great Danes,
great friends.*
—James F. O'Gorman

Contents

Preface	xi
INTRODUCTION	1
NEW YORK CITY, 1847	16
BRUNSWICK, MAINE, 1847–1848	18
NEW HAVEN, CONNECTICUT, 1847–1849	29
HARTFORD, CONNECTICUT, 1849	34
PHILADELPHIA, PENNSYLVANIA, 1849–1850	43
NEW YORK CITY, 1850–1851	49
NORWICHTOWN, CONNECTICUT, 1851–1852	58
NEW YORK CITY, 1853–1860	65
EPILOGUE	96
Appendix: Wheeler's Addresses in the United States	99
Notes	101
Index	111

Preface

Immigration was an important factor in the early development of the architectural profession in the United States. From the arrival on these shores of English-born Benjamin Henry Latrobe in 1796 onward, architects trained elsewhere brought with them direct knowledge of European architecture to supplement the bookish information of local designers and taught the new nation some of the skills necessary to establish professional practice. They in turn needed to adapt to local ways. They came from various regional backgrounds: Ireland (James Hoban), Scotland (John Notman), France (Pierre-Charles L'Enfant, Maximilien Godefroy, Joseph-Francois Mangin, Joseph-Jacques Ramée), Bohemia (Leopold Eidlitz), Schleswig-Holstein (Detlef Lienau), Lombardy (Antonio Mondelli), England (Isaac Holden, John Haviland, Richard Upjohn, Calvert Vaux, as well as Latrobe), and other regions. Some remained for the rest of their lives; others returned home after careers in the States. Among the latter was English-born Gervase Wheeler (1823/25–1889), whose American career stretched from early 1847 to very early 1860. Other English architects who arrived about the same time as Wheeler and stayed to have long careers in New York include Charles Duggin and Alfred J. Bloor.

Until now only the most cursory—and often unstructured or misleading—published information has been available on the course of Wheeler's American sojourn, a frustrating fact for those who study mid-nineteenth-century American architecture. He has not had the historical stature of contemporary architects such as A. J. Davis or writers such as A. J. Downing, and he left only a difficult-to-follow trail of his activities in this country. There is still much we do not know about Wheeler's career, but we do know that it is worth studying. He worked—for good or ill—with Richard Upjohn and Henry Austin. His work was, at least initially, promoted by Andrew Jackson Downing, and he designed such important extant mid-century buildings as the Henry Boody house in Brunswick, Maine, the Patrick Barry house in Rochester, New York, the (now altered) chapel at Williams College in Massachusetts, and many other equally significant works now lost. Wheeler also published two books in the United States, *Rural Homes* (1851) and *Homes for the People* (1855), both of which went through many editions, were much discussed in their own day, and are still the subject of scholarly commentary. He trained Henry Hudson Holly, himself a busy architect and author of several popular books on domestic design. Such a person warrants more detailed attention from historians than he has received.

After an apprenticeship with a major London architect and travel on the Continent, Wheeler arrived in the United States, it seems, as a brash young man: talented, ambitious, a bit disdainful of his provincial peers, manipulative, footloose (either by inclination or necessity), and somewhat devious. He was also charming, cultivated, intelligent, and handsome, according to the evidence at hand. Why he came to this country we do not know; why he left, taking his American wife and several children with him, is a question we can only pose. We are better informed about his professional achievement than about his personal character. In either case we are left with many gaps. Neither portrait nor detailed physical description of Wheeler has surfaced.

This modest guide is intended to organize what we now know about Wheeler's sojourn in America. Certainly future study will fill in many lacunae. The text is arranged chronologically according to places he resided (however briefly in some cases), and is conceived as a springboard for further research. It grows out of Renée Tribert's 1988 M.S. thesis, written under the direction of George E. Thomas at the Graduate Program in Historic Preservation at the University of Pennsylvania, and has been revised by Ms Tribert and James F. O'Gorman on the basis of new research. The original version was prepared with the help of the late John Ward, then a student at Bowdoin College, the late Jill Allibone, an English architectural historian, the staff of the Library Company of Philadelphia, and David G. DeLong of the University of Pennsylvania. To that list should be added Earle G. Shettleworth, Jr., Director of the Maine Historic Preservation Commission, Margaret Coffey of the Berlin Connecticut Congregational Church, Gary Murray and John Shafer, historians of the First Presbyterian Union Church in Owego, New York, Lorna Condon of Historic New England, Christopher Wigren of the Connecticut Trust for Historic Preservation, Jeanne Hablanian of the Art Library, Wellesley College, Michael J. Lewis of Williams College, Jeffery A. Cohen of Bryn Mawr College, Kathleen Curran and Peter J. Knapp at Trinity College, Hartford, Sylvia Kennick Brown, Williams College Archivist, Diane Norman, Otis Library, Norwich, Conn., Anna James of the Lambeth Palace Library, London, Pamela Clark, Registrar of the Royal Archives, Windsor Castle, David Beasley, Librarian of the Goldsmith's Company, London, and Ellenor Alcorn, Philippa Glanville, John Elliott, and Andrew Saint in London. Thanks are also due Sarah Allabach and Michael J. Lewis for their critical reading of an early draft; they are not responsible for the inevitable errors. Wellesley College supported this publication with a Faculty Research Award and a subvention from the McNeil Fund of the Wellesley Art Department facilitated by Alice T. Friedman.

Gervase Wheeler

Introduction

BRITISH BACKGROUND AND LITERARY SOURCES

Sources suggest that Wheeler's family was originally from Margate, Kent, although he was born in St. Pancras, North London. Members of his family were interred at the parish church in Margate, and when Wheeler returned to England after his years in America, he at first took up residence there. His father, also named Gervase, was a manufacturer of gold, silver, and gilt jewelry who worked as the London agent for a Birmingham firm from 1818 to his death in 1840. His shop was located at 28 Bartlett's Buildings in Holborn, according to period London directories.[1] We hear nothing about the younger Wheeler's home life or early education, although growing up in an artisan's household must have predisposed him to a career that was to encompass art, architecture, and decorative and landscape design.

A tantalizing piece of information regarding the elder Wheeler's elevated connections appeared in his son's book *Homes for the People*, where the author mentions his father "building a small cottage on a peculiarly beautiful spot . . . as a suburban estate" from the design of an architect who was to become "one of England's honored names." This may have been the "Elm Villa, Finchley," mentioned in the senior Wheeler's obituary, but lack of corroborating evidence to identify the architect and confirm the statement diminishes its significance. Still, it would, if substantiated, suggest the family's financial and social position, and provide a clearer picture of the younger Wheeler's background. He tells the story not only to demonstrate social position but to emphasize the relationship between dwelling and site, a concern that marked his professional career.

The elder Wheeler had at least one known worthy social connection in Sir Charles Wesley, "Chaplain of St. James and Priest in Ordinary to the Queen."[2] While the nature of the relationship remains unclear, it in due course extended to the entire Wheeler family. It may also suggest, as does the younger Wheeler's ordering of a crucifix when he was working at Bowdoin College, that his religious affiliation was, not surprisingly, Anglican. (Dissenters abhorred the crucifix.) From this likely arose his expectation of obtaining Episcopal commissions in the United States.

Although we can assume that Wheeler was an Anglican, he appears not to have been so narrow-minded as Richard Upjohn (another English immigrant), who once turned down a commission for a Unitarian church because he was

[1]

an Episcopalian.³ Wheeler designed houses of worship for Congregationalists, Presbyterians, and other religious sects.

In 1848, recently arrived in America, Wheeler received a cordial letter from Wesley in answer to one of his own apparently asking for introductions to clerics in his new home. In it, the chaplain mentioned his friendship with the senior Wheeler, and expressed genuinely warm feelings toward the son: "I am very glad to find . . . that you have not forgotten an old friend who often thinks of you."⁴ Wesley continued with his assurance of support: "the personal knowledge I have had of yourself for several years joined with the high opinion I have always entertained of your professional talents would make it a pleasure to me to add my testimony to that of your other friends here in your behalf." Unfortunately, Wesley added, he was unable to assist Wheeler with introductions, since he knew no American clerics, and it is doubtful that the relationship with Wesley served the architect in any measurable way.

Of Wheeler's English training we know most from what he tells us. This has been treated skeptically by scholars,⁵ but some of it is verifiable. The first we hear of his presence in this country is in a letter from New York written by William J. Hoppin, lawyer, art critic, and adviser to Leonard Woods, Jr., president of Bowdoin College. It was addressed to Woods on 8 March 1847, one month after Wheeler's disembarkation. Richard Upjohn's Bowdoin College Chapel, designed in 1844, had reached the stage where discussion had begun about its interior decoration. Hoppin had just met Wheeler, who, Hoppin wrote, "will materially assist us in our inquiries as to the proper mode of decorating the chapel. . . . He has been in the studio of Mr. [R. C.] Carpenter . . . & also with Mr. [A. W. N.] Pugin and is quite familiar with the mode of ornamenting in polychromy so much in vogue in Europe."⁶ Pugin and Carpenter were, of course, both celebrated names in the English Gothic Revival, and, in Carpenter's case, the Cambridge Camden Society and the Ecclesiologist Movement.

Wheeler's apprenticeship under Richard Cromwell Carpenter (1812–55) is certain. It began in 1842 when he was between seventeen and nineteen,⁷ but his reputed work under Augustus W. N. Pugin (1812–52) must be questioned. Studies of Pugin's life and work fail to list Wheeler among his apprentices,⁸ and in an advertising flyer printed for him in Philadelphia in 1850, we read that he had had a "strictly professional education in the office of one of the first Architects of London, [and] the opportunity of witnessing and superintending the erection of some of the largest public and private buildings in Europe"⁹ (see Figure 45). Wheeler seems to have been given to a bit of exaggeration in such statements, but "one" can only refer to Carpenter. He probably mentioned the better-known Pugin to Hoppin as an added endorsement. And it is possible that Wheeler had met Pugin, for the latter was a friend of Carpenter's, and, in early years, an enthusiastic supporter of the Cambridge Society. Both men set the standard of correctness in, especially, ecclesiastical design. It was a good orbit in which to develop.

Following his conversion to Catholicism in 1834, Pugin had embraced the cause of a true Catholic architecture, namely, the "second pointed Gothic." He proclaimed his convictions through the publication of several books, including *The True Principles of Pointed or Christian Architecture* (1841) and *An Apology for the Revival of Christian Architecture in England* (1843). A phrase from Wheeler's later correspondence echoes the sentiment. As he sought to obtain his first known commission in America, at Bowdoin College, he enthusiastically expressed his desire to carry out a "Catholic and correct principle of architectural decorating."[10] The statement clearly indicates familiarity with Pugin's principles, which Wheeler could have gotten, of course, from Pugin's publications rather than from direct contact.

R. C. Carpenter was "the chosen designer" of the Cambridge Camden Society.[11] The association, later called the Ecclesiological Society, shared with Pugin a belief in the Gothic revival as the true mode of architectural expression for ecclesiastical building. The difference in the two arms of the movement lay in their religious affiliations: Pugin was staunchly Roman Catholic, while the Society was Anglican. This divergence in faith led in the mid-1840s to a break between Pugin and the Ecclesiologists.

Carpenter's first church, St. Stephen's at Selly Park Road in Birmingham, was, according to the architectural historian Henry-Russell Hitchcock, "perhaps the most 'correct' example of a fourteenth-century English church model being built in 1841 by an architect other than Pugin,"[12] although Carpenter's exalted position in the Society was not fully entrenched until he received the commission for the church of St. Mary Magdalen, London, in 1849, nearly three years after Wheeler left for America. Since the Wheeler family had Birmingham connections, and the Selly Park Road Church was newly erected at the time the younger Wheeler joined Carpenter, it may have been the impetus that set him on his career path. Under the influence of Pugin, Carpenter had developed skills in decorative arts and polychrome decoration, skills he seems to have passed on to Wheeler. William Hoppin must have found Wheeler's proclaimed expertise in polychrome decorative work convincing, for he wrote to Woods that "his designs for church needlework . . . show considerable power over form and colour in ecclesiastical decoration."[13] But, as we shall see, the ecclesiastical work Wheeler managed to do in America was rather different from that of his mentor.

Wheeler entered the English architectural scene during a period of transition. Practicing architects had begun to recognize the need for standards of professional integrity and work ethics to establish the value of their services in the eyes of the public. While the tradition of apprenticeship persisted, the concern for professionalism led in the 1830s to a surge of schools and professional organizations. These included the Royal Institute of British Architects (R.I.B.A.), established in 1834 to train architects. In the years before mid-century the position of the architect began to reach a level at which it was essential not only to show artistic ability, but "to establish in the public eye [a] professional reputation."[14] Although Wheeler had apprenticed to Carpenter, he advertised his "strictly professional education" in his Philadelphia flyer.

A great part of Wheeler's approach to design can be traced to propriety of architectural expression, the essence of truth and fitness as prescribed by Pugin and his follower in architectural theory, John Ruskin. In *Rural Homes* Wheeler cites the early parts of Ruskin's *Modern Painters* (1843–46); his influential *Seven Lamps of Architecture* (1849) and *Stones of Venice* (1851) came too late to affect Wheeler's training, but they were well-known guides in America during Wheeler's sojourn. Ruskin essentially took the ideals promulgated by the Ecclesiologists and Pugin and refined them into the premises of truth and fitness, applying them not only to church architecture, but to all manifestations of building.[15] Wheeler was not only familiar with these ideas, but later in his career assumed them as his own. The preface to *Rural Homes* ends with the following paragraph:

> [I]n the hope of infusing something of its spirit therein, I have mentally headed every page with a sentence suggested as a matin and even song to every architect and amateur—Mr. Ruskin's great maxim, "Until *common sense* finds its way to architecture, *there can be but little hope for it.*"

A review of that book in *Harper's New Monthly Magazine* considered that Wheeler had indeed "caught something of his [Ruskin's] aesthetic spirit."[16] Wheeler's writings reveal his ongoing concern with Ruskin's principles.

Wheeler was also familiar with the picturesque esthetic. The movement originated in eighteenth-century England. Its intent with regard to domestic architecture was most succinctly defined by Humphrey Repton and Richard Payne Knight as the "characteristicness" of a building to its purpose.[17] A concurrent and newly advocated concern with regard to building design was put forth by Uvedale Price, who suggested planning a building with full consideration of the views and vistas from within. Thus the theory as it evolved encouraged buildings conceived in relation to picturesque landscape and saw the triumph of irregularity and dramatic massing over ordered classicism. Styles, whether Italianate or Gothic, were simply means for expressing the Picturesque.

These ideas, distilled and clarified over time, would inspire men like John Claudius Loudon in Britain and Andrew Jackson Downing in America as they formulated the romantic historicism of the mid-nineteenth century. The domestic work of Wheeler, for the most part rural, was no exception, and derived significantly from this esthetic. Several scholars have noticed this. Henry-Russell Hitchcock pointed to the precedence of the Picturesque in the domestic architectural work of Downing, Davis, Wheeler, and others, ascribing their plans to Picturesque models in Great Britain in the 1830s.[18] He mentioned specifically John White's *Rural Architecture*, published in Glasgow in 1845, as a source for Wheeler, among other architects, "as many of the designs in their books of the [18]50s made evident."[19] Christopher Hussey had already referred to Francis Goodwin's *Rural Architecture* of 1835 for its influence on Wheeler and his contemporaries.[20]

Joseph Gwilt's *Encyclopaedia of Architecture* (1842) is among the reference works Wheeler mentioned in his writings. This provides comprehensive information ranging from history and theory to specifics of practice necessary to the complete understanding of the architectural profession. The introduction admonishes the student to digest thoroughly such a work before assuming the title of architect in good conscience. Wheeler called Gwilt "one of the most useful writers on architectural matters,"[21] and his publications reflect this sentiment, with technical information parallel to that found in the *Encyclopaedia*. The pages of *Rural Homes*, for instance, carry an outline of job specifications, which follows in less detail the order and overall content set out by Gwilt.[22] Although Wheeler's American books advocated a rural esthetic, his instructions for achieving it were extensive and practical. In the words of the couplet he quoted in *Homes for the People*:

> Tis Use alone that sanctifies expense,
> And Splendor borrows all her rays from Sense.[23]

Another author and theorist mentioned by Wheeler is Owen Jones, who, best known for his work on polychrome decoration, in 1851 achieved fame for his "parti-coloring" of the Crystal Palace in London. An article in the May 1851 issue of *The Bulletin of the American Art Union* examined Jones's work at the Crystal Palace.[24] Wheeler cited this article and described Jones's two-tone wall treatments as an introduction to his own discussion of the decoration of domestic rooms in *Rural Homes*, published the same year.[25] Questions of interior decorating and polychrome engaged Wheeler from the outset of his career; his first projects in America were in these areas.

Wheeler's sources were not limited to his contemporaries; he also referred to historical architectural treatises. In *Homes for the People* he related the story of Phidias and Alcames from the pages of J. F. Blondel's *Cours d'Architecture* (1777).[26] Blondel, an eighteenth-century theorist and teacher, appreciated the truthful representation of the classical style. He found in the tale of Phidias, a

Greek sculptor of the fifth century B.C., and his protege Alcames, an example of the fundamental skills and understanding required to effect truthful representation. Wheeler must have seen in Blondel's reference a parallel to his own understanding of reality and truth in art, and rather immodestly compared himself to Phidias. This concern was consistent with Ruskin's philosophy of truth and fitness, to which Wheeler claimed to adhere. He also read *Le vite de' più celebri architetti* (1768) of Francesco Milizia, probably, although not necessarily, in the English translation of 1826, and cites the Roman's remark about the ancients accomplishing great works by "producing a grand impression at the first glance."[27] He might have equated that with Ruskin's "Lamp of Power."

Wheeler was aware of the writings of his American architectural peers too. As we shall see, he certainly knew Downing's publications and perhaps Downing himself. Among others he mentions the "brilliant writer and most accomplished Southern architect," Robert Cary Long of Baltimore, whose "Architectonics" articles in the *Literary World* (1848–49) he cites concerning the scale of decorative details.[28] In several instances in *Rural Homes* he made use of the findings of Dr. Luther Bell of the McLean Asylum for the Insane in Boston, who in 1848 published a treatise on the importance of adequate ventilation and practical applications to achieve it. In both his American books Wheeler applied the information to his residential designs.[29]

A passage from a book entitled *Rural Hours* (1850), the work of "a lady" (in fact Susan Fenimore Cooper), published less than a year earlier than *Rural Homes*, gave Wheeler an opportunity for oblique commentary on the merits of American architecture.[30] Wheeler concurred with Cooper's negative assessment of the American tendency to mimic architecture, which resulted in many homes of the exact same pattern. By pulling this selection into his own work, he strengthened his argument for customized, place-based, picturesque domestic designs. Wheeler also mentioned the popular reminiscence of America by Fredrika Bremer, *The Homes of the New World*, in *Homes for the People*.[31] He quotes Downing's complaints about Bremer's deploring the newness and littleness of American buildings. He countered with remarks about their convenience and comfort, qualities he emphasized in his other writings about the contrast between American and English architecture.

Wheeler's reading ranged from the practical to the philosophical. Among the latter works, in the last chapter of *Rural Homes* (entitled "Rural Architecture as a Fine Art") he cites at length the Scotsman Henry Home, Lord Kames's, *Elements of Criticism* (1762) on the matter of taste. "Undoubtedly there exists a rule or standard in nature for trying individual tastes," he writes, "and . . . after a time the search . . . must be eventually successful."[32] According to Kames and other Scottish thinkers, there exists an "absolute or intrinsic beauty," which Wheeler says can be blunted and must be strengthened "by education and important refinement." The influence of the Scottish Enlightenment on the art of the United States is now beyond dispute.[33]

The literature Wheeler read also included many of the English and American periodicals of the day. Judging from references throughout his books, he was interested in an extensive range of topics. It can be inferred from his citations of articles that while in America he remained familiar with British trends in art and architecture through the weekly *Art Journal* and *The Mechanics' Magazine* of London.[34] *Sartain's Union Magazine*, the *New York Tribune*, and the New York issue of *Literary World* provided sources for more general current information and critical analysis from the American perspective.[35] Wheeler probably also occasionally read journals such as the *London Literary World* and *The Builder*, and *The Home Journal* published in New York, since they carried reviews of his work or in some cases his written contributions.

In the references noted above, Wheeler usually specified the sources of his remarks. Comparison of the various passages indicates that, while he readily used the information as the basis for his own arguments, he neither misrepresented nor plagiarized to fit his own requirements. But a review of *Homes for the People* printed in *The Builder* in 1855 contended that Wheeler had blatantly plagiarized another's work. It has not been possible within the scope of this overview of his American years to assess the degree of plagiarism on Wheeler's part in his several literary efforts. We might note, however, that contrary to the impression conveyed by the disdain of the British reviewer, such lifting of material remained a common practice before the institution of international copyright laws in the nineteenth century.

Wheeler's early experience was not limited to England or to publications. His Philadelphia advertising flyer mentions "witnessing and superintending of some of the largest public and private buildings in Europe."[36] This sounds a bit like a puff, but references can be found throughout his *Rural Homes* to the architecture as well as the art galleries of the Continent. England, France, and Germany, he wrote, "abound with charming cottages, entrance lodges, and manorial . . . residences constructed of . . . [brick]; see Holland House, l'Hotel Choiseul, or the innumerable pretty things about the sunny lawns of Western Germany."[37] This smacks of direct contact rather than armchair travel. It has been said that his first American work at Bowdoin College strongly suggests that he had studied in Munich,[38] although his apprenticeship with Carpenter may have been sufficient in that regard. As he tells us in his *Homes for the People*, he had again made a "recent visit to Europe," probably in late 1852-early 1853.[39] His comments do not explain the purpose of his travels, but he seems to have learned enough German, Spanish, and Italian to have translated lyrics written in these languages for New

York music publishers.[40] None of this information is extensive, but whatever experience he may have had abroad, combined with his training in London, presumably provided him with a broader view of the range and possibilities of design than many American architects had at mid-century.

By the time he arrived in America, then, young Wheeler had benefited from thorough training in England and had traveled on the Continent. He had crowded much into his preparatory years and was better and more broadly prepared for his profession than the typical American designer who rose from the ranks of the builders. In *Rural Homes* he called such a man an "archy-tect."[41] That condescending attitude may have been a cause of trouble among his peers.

AMERICAN CONTEXT

Directions evident in mid-century American society, such as the ideal of individual freedom and a preference for innovation and progress, manifested themselves in contemporary architectural theory. Building upon the precepts of the Picturesque, the British writer John Claudius Loudon, and themes of the individual as expounded by American contemporaries such as Ralph Waldo Emerson, Andrew Jackson Downing (1815–52) believed that domestic architecture should represent and transmit the republican political values of American society and the aspirations of the individual owner. His theory asserted that the essence of the American domestic experience was rural or suburban, and largely catered to those who could afford country homes near the great American cities. Wheeler, though British, would nonetheless reflect this middle-class American trend in both his buildings and his books.

As would be expected of a mid-century architect of chiefly rural homes, Wheeler frequently cited Downing's contributions in both landscape and architecture and found his own work featured in Downing's publications. Wheeler's remarks complemented the advances toward picturesque expression in domestic design made possible as a result of Downing's efforts. He referred his readers to Downing's "excellent" works, which would help keep them from "prettiness, whimsicality and the false picturesque" in cottage design (implying that his own understanding of the subject was total and intuitive). In his discussion of residential gardens, the ambience of picturesque buildings, Wheeler deferred not only to Downing but to Patrick Barry, a leading horticulturist and pomologist, noting selections from his *Fruit Garden* (1851).[42] He would later have a hand in the design of Barry's house at Rochester, New York.

Wheeler arrived in America at a time when these notions were finding voice. He came with grounding in the environment that had created the Picturesque esthetic. His initial contributions to *The Horticulturist* prove an acquaintanceship with Downing at the latest by 1849, but his role in developing the latter's theories was negligible; Downing had been exploring the Picturesque for a decade. As this evolving theory was applied to design, it drew heavily from British precedents. Downing translated the revised view of architecture into statements of form associated with the British Picturesque: the house was to relate to its setting, the plan was to be a diagram of use, the elevation adapted to the needs of the plan, and the whole defined by the character of the owner. In implementing these ideas, American architects such as John Notman, Richard Upjohn, and A. J. Davis would no longer restrict themselves to the vocabulary of the waning Grecian revival. They sought alternative stylistic expressions. The result was a flourishing of other revival modes—Gothic, Tudor, Moorish, Roman, or Tuscan—applied in a manner as befitted the situation and the client.

Wheeler's contribution to American domestic architecture was primarily in writings and published designs that propagated the Picturesque point of view. He shared with Downing an approach to the explanation and application of the Picturesque based in each case on British antecedents. While the vast majority of American architectural texts up to this period clung to the format of the traditional builders' guides, Downing and Wheeler presented their ideas in essays addressed to the general public. Downing's *Architecture of Country Houses* (1850) discusses a philosophy of architecture accompanied by renderings by contemporary architects, particularly A. J. Davis, and, in two instances, Wheeler.

Wheeler published *Rural Homes* one year after Downing's book. Its author's comfortable knowledge of the Picturesque vocabulary enabled smooth integration of designs with text. In the book's readable chapters, Wheeler conveyed the essence of the Picturesque in the choice and construction of a residence. The designs were his own, and were intended only as models. Despite giving detailed technical explanations, in which he displayed ease, Wheeler emphasized that an owner should engage an architect for the actual execution of any of his designs because of the need to tailor the house to its intended site. In this way, he joined contemporaries such as the Philadelphia architect Samuel Sloan in promoting to the general public not only himself but also the young architectural profession.[43]

The subsequent editions of *Rural Homes, Homes for the People*, published in 1855 with additional issues to 1868, and republication of Wheeler's writings in general distribution periodicals, followed Downing in spreading information regarding the new domestic architecture. Reviews and advertisements for Wheeler's works appeared not only locally in New York, but throughout the Northeast, in Philadelphia, Rochester, Albany, Hartford, and even as far afield as the Midwest. The editor of the *Genessee Farmer*, a popular magazine for the gentleman agriculturalist published in Rochester, New York, for example, responded in 1852 to a correspondent in Illinois with a recommendation that he read *Rural Homes*. By the time he left the States, Wheeler could be cited, without even mentioning the titles of his books, as *the* authority on the "great laws of fitness" and the congruence of architecture and landscape.[44] His reputation as an architect had reached a very broad audience. His fame nearly rivaled Downing's.

The responsibility of the architect was by no means strictly defined in the 1840s and 1850s. Although the situation was clearer at mid-century than it had been during Benjamin Henry Latrobe's American career, the American client was still loath to recognize the difference the architect drew between himself and the master builder. The master builder, in turn, resisted the encroachment on his trade. The frustrations felt by the architect as a result of this ambiguity were magnified for an English-trained architect like Wheeler. An anonymous architect, quoted by Constance Greiff in her monograph on John Notman, complained in 1834 that "the US offered the potential for economic improvement, but little comprehension of the role of the professional."[45] From the outset of his career in America, Wheeler considered himself a professional. The first documented correspondence from him, in 1847, is signed "Gervase Wheeler, Architect."[46] This self-assurance on the part of one so young may have accounted for some of the tensions evident during Wheeler's stay in America.

It was not until 1857, ten years after Wheeler's arrival in this country, that a group of men gathered in New York to attempt for the second time to create a professional body, the American Institute of Architects (A.I.A.). Thirteen practitioners, led by Richard Upjohn, agreed to the aims of the society and invited "other reputable members of the profession" to a meeting to adopt a constitution.[47] Attendees included Calvert Vaux and Frederick C. Withers (also English immigrants), John Notman, Thomas U. Walter, A. J. Davis, and seven others. Wheeler, though known personally by Upjohn and by reputation through his books by many of the others, was not in that group, nor did his name appear among its membership during his remaining years in America. Wheeler's absence from the rolls is significant. A man who claimed a high level of proficiency and professionalism, as he often did in his printed work and undoubtedly in person, would hardly have declined to seek membership in such an association (we will see that he later joined the R.I.B.A.). We must conclude that his peers, especially Upjohn, who eventually came to mistrust the man, either did not consider him or did not accept him. Membership in the A.I.A. was contingent on the "honorable practice" of the profession. Candidates for membership had to be nominated by two existing members and voted on by the remaining body; three negative votes were sufficient to blackball an architect.[48]

The newly established A.I.A. sought to encourage the education of its members in artistic and technical matters, and to educate the general public in the significance of architecture and the role of the architect. The extent of an architect's control over design and construction, and the matter of fees, were often points of contention, and were among the first issues the A.I.A. attempted to resolve. In the early years of the organization, members could not agree upon a schedule of fixed rates for architectural services. Some of the more prominent architects had attempted to standardize the rate of compensation. By the late 1840s, John Notman, in an effort to define professional procedures, sought a 5 percent commission on buildings that he supervised. He was not always successful.[49] Similarly, Richard Upjohn established an average fee of 5 percent, but often had to dispute the rate with clients.[50] Upjohn was among those, including Richard Morris Hunt and Isaiah Rogers, who took their cases to court for settlement in the 1840s and 1850s.[51] Wheeler also experienced difficulties in this area.

The first indication that Wheeler had codified his fees can be found in his Philadelphia advertising flyer.[52] His terms were "Three per cent upon all buildings within the city," and "Five per cent, upon the amount expended for full professional services upon all buildings within 50 miles of the city," beyond which expenses would accrue. Much the same appears on a letterhead he used in 1857.[53] The latter postdates some of the litigation on the issue by his peers, and may reflect Wheeler's confidence in the possibilities of obtaining such compensation, although it would appear that he rarely did.

He seems to have contented himself with flat rates. In 1848 he was voted $100 by the Governing Board of Bowdoin College to design a new President's House, though it was never executed. With the design of a new corporate office for the Insurance Company of North America, in Philadelphia, Wheeler asked for the "regular charge of 3% on the cost," but was paid $75, which represented less than 2 percent of the final tally.[54] The documentation on the Patrick Barry House commission in Rochester, and the erection of Goodrich Hall, the chapel at Williams College, indicate that again Wheeler received a flat fee for delivery of the design drawings. The Barry House cost approximately $27,500 to erect, but the Ellwanger and Barry nursery journals record a $95 payment to the architect, less than one half a percent on the cost of construction.[55] At Williams College, the information is incomplete, but Wheeler apparently received a one-time payment of $250.[56] It should be said that in all these cases it appears that Wheeler received payment only for drawings, not for supervision.

Although what evidence we have suggests that Wheeler did not often supervise the buildings he drew, in the Philadelphia flyer he says that "various buildings... have been constructed from his designs and under his personal superintendence, [and] he has the satisfaction of knowing that the estimated outlay has in no case been greatly exceeded." He goes on to say that this fact can be confirmed by "gentlemen of influence concerned in their erection." As so often is the case, we have here only Wheeler's word, and that word can be seen at times to have been a bit inflated, and in this case especially, for he had been in the country for only three years when the flyer was printed.

Wheeler also tried another option for his professional services. In 1852 he advertised in *The Genessee Farmer* for commission work and offered to supply "such information as can be given by letter" for $2.[57] The type of information to be provided is unclear, but Wheeler may have considered this approach a means of reaching potential clients or merely of padding a thin purse.

The A.I.A. discussed not only questions of client-architect relationship and fees, but the ethics of the profession itself. A code of ethics was not in fact promulgated until the early twentieth century, but the issues probably had their genesis in the years leading up to the association. Areas of concern included undercutting fees and slighting other architects' reputation or work. From the outset Wheeler seemed to typify the very deportment the society castigated. During his engagement at Bowdoin in 1847–48, he not only criticized Upjohn's work but offered his own services for areas of alleged deficiency on Upjohn's part. He later tried to interfere with Upjohn's church in Norwich, Connecticut. Correspondence in the latter case indicates Upjohn's indignation against Wheeler, and such behavior perhaps later kept him out of the A.I.A.

Exclusion from the American Institute of Architects may have had an adverse impact on Wheeler's career. The lack of documentation uncovered for the period makes any realistic assessment of his success tenuous. However, Wheeler's last known significant commissions occurred in 1857 (the year of the Institute's formation), with the Patrick Barry House and Goodrich Hall at Williams College, in Williamstown, Massachusetts; in 1858 his landscape design entry for Bushnell Park, in Hartford, Connecticut, won first place, but was never executed. His return to England in the earliest days of 1860 may have been precipitated in whole or in part by his lack of collegial acceptance in this country.

PERSONAL AFFAIRS

Documents relating to Wheeler's personal life in America are as difficult to find as those relating to his English upbringing. Here too most of what we can deduce about such matters comes from his own writings, often by reading between the lines of either published documents or the occasional surviving letter.

The first years of Wheeler's stay in America seem to have been marked by poor health. He alluded to his difficulties regularly. In December 1847, "ill health which for some time confined me to the house" detained him from his duties with regard to the library decoration at Bowdoin College.[58] The following May, he complained of "a return of my attacks, the liability of reoccurrence of which will forever prevent my enjoying in any laborious or sedentary pursuit."[59] That same month, "an unfortunate severe pain in my side" again meant that he could not work as much as hoped.[60]

His problems did not relent as the year passed, for in September, having relocated to New Haven, Wheeler complained that "the weather is bitterly cold and I being (and have been for some time) very unwell with continual attacks of cold on my chest and dysentery, feel it very much."[61] Two months later, in November 1848, he again lamented: "I am sorry to say I have been really ill, and have more than once arranged a change of scene for a while and each time been frustrated by bad health."[62] Dysentery was not uncommon in the nineteenth century. The early descriptions of Wheeler's symptoms indicate that it may have been the cause of his troubles from the outset. How he fared in later years has not been recorded. Though Wheeler's poor health during this time is clear, the severity and frequency with which he was affected are subject to doubt. His statements were invariably made within the context of work, and often have a pitiable tone to them, as though they were convenient excuses for not having prepared a design in a timely fashion. The remarks hint at a manipulative nature.

Wheeler arrived in America a bachelor, but seems soon to have met his future wife. He wrote to the Reverend Leonard Woods in Brunswick, Maine, in May 1848, a year after his disembarkation at New York, expressing, in good Victorian fashion, the hope

> that once I am in my new and sacred relations to gain a friend who will never change and a support which will never fail and that I may be able to make myself worthy of them and may draw peace and happiness from the directing influence of the other.[63]

Charles Wesley's letter of later that year related how Wheeler's mother had "hinted something which we were all especially anxious to hear more of."[64] Although vague, these oblique references may suggest that he was affianced soon after his arrival, and in any event he married Catherine ("Kate") Brewer Hyde in New York City on 18 September 1850.[65] His bride was born about 1833 in Connecticut, perhaps in Norwich or Norwichtown where the architect later briefly lived and worked, making her roughly a decade younger than her husband. Over the years the couple had eight children, five born in New York City.[66]

What information we have about Wheeler as an individual presents him as intelligent, charming, and devious. Comments made during Wheeler's career by those he encountered paint the same initial impression of an educated, refined man. Though for the most part concerned with questions of professional ability, William Hoppin of New York, Wheeler's first known contact, seemed impressed with his knowledge and manners. Discussing polychrome work for the Bowdoin College Chapel, he wrote that Wheeler's "information respecting it is extensive and accurate and accompanied furthermore with much taste and discrimination."[67] Hoppin later expressed his confidence in Wheeler, noting "I think I should have been able to detect any considerable disparity between his powers and his pretensions."[68] A few years later, in December 1849, when Wheeler was in Philadelphia, he dined with a prospective client, Henry Fisher, and his brother Sidney. Sidney described Wheeler in his diary as "young, good looking, of gentlemanlike manners and appearance and converses with ease and elegance. His mind is evidently cultivated and he has a taste for literature and art."[69] This aspect of his character was manifest during his career in the social position of his acquaintances and clients, and in his own literary work.

While Wheeler seemed able to charm some people upon meeting them, a lack of discretion in financial and other matters sometimes led to strained relations. His living habits, suited to city life, caused embarrassment in the small New England town of Brunswick where he undertook his first commission. As early as September 1847, the Reverend Woods lamented Wheeler's handling of money matters and his "want of gentlemanly propriety" in this regard.[70] Some months later, in February 1848, an uncomfortable situation arose in settling Wheeler's room bill. He had spent considerably more in living expenses than the arrangement with the trustees of the college had called for. While he recognized the "somewhat more expensive scale than the committee . . . might have deemed necessary," he did little to alleviate the problem.[71] Wheeler was also manipulative in his dealings with people. When the matter of expenses came up, he pleaded his case by implying that he had been "unduly influenced by the inducements held out . . . for the future."[72] He was referring to the commission for the interior design of the chapel, which was never given to him, contingent upon approval of his work in the library. On another occasion, when Woods was in Boston on business, Wheeler wrote him to ask that he purchase a crucifix. He cleverly referred to his pro bono commission for the library interior, knowing the effect it would have: "I do not mean that I am making certain drawings for this, or that this would be considered a return for them . . . [but such a gesture] would amply compensate for this expenditure of time and skill on my part."[73]

Wheeler seems to have been given to exaggeration as well. This tendency was manifest particularly as he sought to impress contacts and prospective clients. When he met the Fishers in Philadelphia, Wheeler mentioned his acquaintance with Currer Bell, the author, he said, of *Jane Eyre*, and divulged "that these works were chiefly written by his sister Ann Bell." An undated marginal gloss alongside the entry in Sidney Fisher's diary notes that Wheeler was an imposter: Fisher evidently found out that Bell was in fact the pseudonym of Charlotte Brontë. The same entry had noted that "he knows also Miss Bremer now in this country, a Swedish lady," though no marginalia accompanied the statement.[74] Perusal of Bremer's writings yielded no notice of Gervase Wheeler, though she did mention her meetings with A. J. Downing.

The above information derives almost entirely from correspondence in the first years of Wheeler's career in America. It is impossible to know whether he changed over time. But whatever his character flaws, Wheeler must have had an engaging personality. He associated throughout his residence in America, at least in a business capacity, with socially prominent people, as the following outline of the years 1847 to 1860 will reveal.

New York City, 1847

Gervase Wheeler disembarked at New York from the *General Victoria* out of London on 10 February 1847. The passenger list gives an estimate of his year of birth as 1823 and his age as 24, although the 1881 English census gives his age then as 56 thus making his year of birth 1825 and his age on arrival in the United States 22. According to a list of embarking passengers published in the *New York Times* for 9 January 1860, he had just left New York for Southampton on the steamship *Arago*.[1] So we now have the precise limits of his nearly 13-year stay in the New World between the ages of 22 or 24 and 36 or 38. In seeking a foothold in the emerging profession in the new country, he flitted for seven years or so from place to place in New England (and Philadelphia), finally settling in New York City in 1853. During his stay he practiced as artist, architect, and landscape designer, as well as author.[2] He had significant success; he also made some people unhappy.

Within a month of his arrival in New York Wheeler had the good fortune to meet William J. Hoppin, a lawyer and adviser to the Reverend Leonard J. Woods, the president of Bowdoin College in Brunswick, Maine. On 8 March Hoppin wrote to Woods to say that "a young Englishman by the name of Gervase Wheeler was introduced to me the other day. . . . As he has but lately arrived [he] has to make a name for himself."[3] Hoppin was well educated, with degrees from Yale, Middlebury, and Harvard, and had been a founder of the Century Club in New York. A frequent traveler to Europe, he eventually resided in London from 1876 to 1886 as secretary of the U.S. Legation. Hoppin's activities indicate that his primary interest was the art world. By 1850 he was a member of the Committee of Management of the American Art Union, and the new editor of the organization's bulletin. He was thus well prepared to judge the newcomer's qualifications. Although there is no documentation to confirm a continued relationship between the two, it is likely that Wheeler cultivated one. He not only began his American sojourn in New York, but later practiced there for over six years.

By April 1847 Wheeler had taken rooms at 29 Greenwich Street in the city.[4] At first, he sought to make a name for himself by turning away from the more practical aspects of engineering and architecture, instead promoting his skills at interior design, particularly in polychrome decoration, skills he must have gained under Carpenter and with an eye on Pugin. In a letter to the Reverend Woods, Richard Upjohn, the English immigrant architect whom Wheeler must have immediately looked up, noted that Wheeler desired "to turn his attention exclusively to decorative art."[5] The 1847 catalogue of an exhibition at the National Academy of Design in New York City includes the following entry for Wheeler: "#371. Section of a Room with Gothic Furniture."[6] As we shall see, his first documented commission was for the interior decoration of the library incorporated within the chapel at Bowdoin College, although much to Upjohn's chagrin, he also tried to meddle in other parts of the building.

During the summer of 1847 Wheeler traveled through New England, particularly Connecticut, perhaps as part of his courting of Catherine, and established a relationship with Henry Austin, a New Haven architect. According to Wheeler, the two were to join in business as of the first of September. In correspondence with Woods at the time, Wheeler implied a certain success in obtaining commissions, as he wrote: "I am happy to say I have so much to do both presently and in future I can afford to undertake a little 'fancy work.'"[7] It is difficult to see now on what he based this optimism. This may have been an artifice for convincing prospective clients, perhaps even himself, of his hoped-for success in America. For having announced a wealth of upcoming work, and an engagement with Austin, he proceeded on a speculative gamble to Brunswick, a commercial, manufacturing, and college town where he remained at least until May of the following year — some ten months. His work there was paid for only sparingly by the client, as he knew it would be.

Brunswick, Maine, 1847–1848

LIBRARY DECORATION, BOWDOIN COLLEGE CHAPEL

The "fancy work" mentioned in Wheeler's letter refers to the interior decoration of the Bowdoin Chapel building, and marks another strategy by which Wheeler sought to establish himself in America. In this instance, he offered his services at cost in order to be given the opportunity of proving himself. He agreed to furnish colored drawings for the decoration of the library in the Chapel building, and to supervise their execution, in return for reimbursement of his expenses only.

Reverend Woods oversaw the design and construction of the Chapel.[1] From the outset, the building was to serve the usual religious function, and to contain as well an art gallery, library, and president's office. A theologian and teacher, well read and well traveled, and knowledgeable about the latest European trends in art and architecture, Woods was convinced of the appropriateness of polychrome for the decoration of the Chapel interior.

The contract for the design of the building itself had been awarded to Richard Upjohn, and construction begun in 1845. In response to the multiple uses of the building, Upjohn planned a double-spired design based on the German *Rundbogenstil*, with a large Romanesque hall flanked by separate art gallery and library, to be constructed of granite quarried locally. As for the interior design, contrary to Wood's own aspirations, Upjohn wanted the walls to be pale, subdued, and without figured polychrome. Woods sought Hoppin's advice on the matter. He hoped to find support for his idea of a colorful interior, and wondered whether it was within the limits of propriety to consult another architect for this aspect of the design. Hoppin, in the letter introducing Wheeler to Woods, confirmed that the newcomer "will materially assist us in our inquiries as to the proper mode of decorating the Chapel at Brunswick. . . . He is certain that it [polychrome] will increase rather than diminish the solemnity of the effect of your Chapel."[2] By July, Woods had interviewed and clearly been impressed by Wheeler, particularly as Wheeler favored just that method of decoration that Woods so longed to display at Bowdoin. Upjohn at this time was still being recalcitrant about adopting any coloring for the Chapel, but had agreed to draw up some designs, though Woods considered, on what evidence we do not know, that "nothing . . . will come up to the standard of Mr. Wheeler."[3]

Richard Upjohn's English background was in cabinetmaking and carpentry. He arrived in America in 1829 and belonged to an older generation than Wheeler, having progressed from craftsman to architect without the benefit of a formal professional education. At the time of his commission at Bowdoin, he was still trying to establish and define his role as architect with much difficulty in a profession as yet in its infancy.[4] There can be little doubt that he resented the interference of the young newcomer, and perhaps even more the fact that Woods had challenged his authority on the job by seeking outside advice.

Wheeler was very interested in the possibility presented by the President, not only as a step toward establishing a reputation, but as an opportunity to demonstrate the type of architectural decoration then fashionable in England and Europe. As the art historian Kathleen Curran has written, this was an extraordinary undertaking in this time and place, based on London and Munich precedents, by an unproven artist.[5] As a result, Wheeler agreed "in the most generous way" to submit renderings, "and superintend their execution, making no other charge than for his mere expenses."[6] Wheeler's amiability in this exchange had the desired effect; Woods thereafter chose to employ the services of both Upjohn and Wheeler. It was a decision unlikely to produce harmony.

Aware of the potential awkwardness of such a situation, Woods once again appealed to Hoppin for advice. The men agreed that "Mr. U. is so sensitive upon this point that if he should know it was projected, he would throw up the whole affair."[7] Woods wondered whether Wheeler's qualifications vindicated such an intervention:

> [H]ow far should we be justified by custom, by common opinion, and strict propriety, in adopting a style of decoration not recommended by the architect? . . . [W]ould it be safe for us, if we approved of Mr. Wheeler's designs, and felt authorized to adopt them, to entrust the execution of them to him? His scientific attainments, and his fine taste, cannot be doubted; but has he experience enough to entitle him to perfect confidence in introducing a new style which will be open to every species of criticism?[8]

As a cautionary move, Woods proposed that Wheeler be hired to design the decoration of the library (named Banister Hall in 1850) as an experiment prior to making any decision regarding the Chapel proper.

Hoppin responded to Woods's query by attempting to balance the abilities of each architect against the requirements of the job. He declared that from an ethical standpoint, Upjohn should have the option to submit the first design, but, in the event that the college committee rejected it, another architect's rendering could be adopted. The alternate architect of course would be Wheeler, for Hoppin knew "no other person in the country as competent to carry them out."[9] Woods was sufficiently informed about the profession to question the areas of responsibility subject to an architect's control, and to recognize that the consultation of another architect might be considered a transgression. And in his reply Hoppin admitted being "unable to come to a decision entirely satisfactory to myself." But the hesitation went no further.

By mid-September 1847, Wheeler had met Woods in New York City and together they traveled to Brunswick. The fact that Wheeler took the commission, even on such a tentative program, showed a disregard for the circumstances of his fellow architect. With all due consideration for his own needs, the ease with which he accepted the work, knowing of Upjohn's commitment to the project, reflected a lack of professional deference. In Brunswick Wheeler took up residence in a boarding house run by a Miss Weld at 7 Federal Street on the understanding that he would remain in town some four to six weeks to accomplish his task, now defined as the design of the decoration of the library (Figure 1).[10] In the event that the latter was well received, and pending Upjohn's agreement, he would have the opportunity of focusing on the interior of the Chapel as well.

Wheeler was not content simply to put forth his proposals for decorating the library. He also felt compelled, not always in the most tactful way, to express his views on the work that had already been planned by Upjohn for the Chapel itself. Wheeler regarded uniformity of mode to be extremely important in the overall development of the structure. As Upjohn had designed the chapel in a Romanesque style, Wheeler thought that the detailing throughout should be consistent and of "characteristic ornament." He communicated his reservations about Upjohn's use of Gothic motifs in the interior design to Hoppin who in turn conveyed them to Woods: "Mr. U. has introduced many details in the pointed style and Mr. Wheeler desires you to understand that he should materially vary his designs if any thing besides the Romanesque should be used."[11]

Later remarks by Wheeler expressed more blatantly his disapproval not only of Upjohn's decorative scheme but of his architecture as well. Shortly after his arrival in Brunswick, he wrote that the existing proposals for the Chapel showed a lack of understanding of the principles of honest architecture and "unity of effect," both concepts integral to the ideas of Pugin, Carpenter, and other Gothic revivalists. The construction included "a mass of workmanship useless for purposes of strength" and interior details designed in such a way as insufficiently to "allow of the play of light and shade."[12] Another bold criticism followed closely on the last, this time relative to the architecture of the library. Wheeler submitted remarks on the first of October to the effect that "a very important disadvantage will be found if the work be carried out in the manner there indicated" in Upjohn's drawings.[13] Again, the complaints had mainly to do with the play of light, which was hindered, according to Wheeler, by the heaviness of the balusters and

Figure 1.
*Richard Upjohn, Library,
Bowdoin College Chapel Building,
Brunswick, Maine, 1844–55.
(Courtesy the Maine Historic
Preservation Commission.)*

floors of the upper gallery. He went so far as to offer his own services should the committee agree with his assessment.

Such criticism by a young architect of the work of a senior was not only uncommon but also destructive. In Wheeler's case, it may have been a mark of his own self-conscious sense of education and training compared to his American counterparts, including Upjohn. The critique represented a poor sense of ethics and suggests the root of Wheeler's future problems in this country. The unsolicited advice caused dissention and discomfort among members of the committee and, quite naturally, undermined Wheeler's relationship to Upjohn, although the expression of the latter was slow in coming.

While correspondence from Upjohn to Wheeler has not been discovered, a letter written later that month by Wheeler indicates his attempt to reconcile with Upjohn. After providing him with a lengthy description of his design for the library decoration, Wheeler applauded the overall effect of the Chapel and closed with the following paragraph:

> I am sure that you will approve of what is being done in the Library and I am equally sure that you will do me the justice to say so, and to acquit me of any intention in this matter to act otherwise than in the most perfect good faith toward yourself.[14]

The episode hints at Wheeler's manipulative character. Having interfered in Upjohn's work, he sought to clear himself by appealing to Upjohn's good nature. How effectively relations were smoothed over remains a question, but Wheeler apparently thought that any unpleasantness had been resolved. In January 1848, he noted, "I am glad that Mr. Upjohn seems amiable and shall be pleased to put myself in communication with him on the subject of the Chapel when the time comes."[15] In later letters to Upjohn, Wheeler mentions the older architect's kindnesses, and this suggests either that the rift between the two at the time Wheeler left Brunswick has been exaggerated or that Wheeler was accomplished at denial. It is difficult to gauge with accuracy the implications of the situation, for while Wheeler appears to have acted aggressively and somewhat dishonestly, general correspondence indicates that Upjohn's dealings with the college were marked by tension as well. Certainly part of the trouble may be attributed to the lingering obstinacy of the client, typical for the period, in his unwillingness to yield full control to the architect.

By October 1847, the work on the polychrome decoration of the library had begun.[16] Later in the month Wheeler submitted a description of his project to Upjohn. Ceiling, walls, hood moulds, arches, and columns were to be covered with decoration in "fresco" (on the plaster) and tempera (on the wood).[17] The scheme was a complex one, and the design was not completed until December.

Wheeler described the decoration in detail in a report to the committee: each surface area was treated somewhat differently, but all shared a palette of deep, rich colors: dark red, warm gold, blue, subdued golden brown, and "shades of colour from warm and brightest white and deepest shadow."[18] The interior of the library has since been remodeled, and Wheeler's work has been obscured; though it may still be possible through paint analysis to recapture at least a portion of the polychrome design.

With work under way in the library, Wheeler pursued his campaign of interference in the interior of the Chapel itself. In February 1848 he submitted a proposal to Dr. Woods and the committee. He seems to have been encouraged, as he was engaged to prepare drawings in May.[19] Wheeler did not remain in Brunswick to see that his plans were carried out. During that winter he caused a rift between Woods and himself, the exact nature of which is not clear—the skimpy documentation suggests a combination of a woman (his landlady, Miss Weld) and a loan of money—and no more is heard about Wheeler as decorator in Brunswick after the spring of 1848. He left a poor reputation in the town, with Woods thinking he had misrepresented himself, and as we shall see, this would come back to haunt him.

Construction of the College Chapel took 11 years to complete. In 1851, when Wheeler had left Brunswick and assumed other commissions in Connecticut and Pennsylvania, an article in the *Bulletin of the American Art Union* reviewed the interior polychrome of Banister Hall. The work was considered "very successful both in form and color," and it was suggested that the designs for the Chapel prepared by Wheeler, if carried out, "would be even more extensively admired."[20] For unknown reasons, his design was never executed.

PROJECT FOR THE PRESIDENT'S HOUSE, BOWDOIN COLLEGE

Wheeler's time in Brunswick was not entirely consumed by work in the Chapel building. He also accepted commissions to design at least two residences, including one for the president of the College. The original president's house had burned in 1839. In November of 1847, the Governing Board of Bowdoin voted $100 to pay for the design of a new house.[21] The decision to rebuild after so many years had no doubt much to do with the fact that Reverend Woods was president. In an undated statement he noted that following his initial negotiations with Wheeler for the Chapel, he had suggested that he "might obtain one or two jobs with which he might be able to clear his expenses."[22] The President's House may have been one such job, for Woods asked the architect to prepare drawings for it.

We know he submitted alternate proposals, but there is no evidence that either design was executed and details about them are minimal. All that is known is that the Board accepted one for a house with tower and two dining rooms en suite for entertaining.[23] One would like to think that the "Villa in the Tudor Style" published in *The Horticulturalist* for June 1849 (see Figure 9) somewhat reflects that design, but there is no evidence to confirm it.

The debate over compensation for this project discloses the concept of the architect that was rooted in Wheeler's British training. He was having financial difficulties and tried to offset his expenses with the income from this commission. He had submitted rough sketches, with the intention of producing full drawings once the design choice had been made. The committee frowned at paying the allotted $100 for such work. In the letter in which he described his projects, Wheeler responded:

> Though I do not pretend to say the drawings are worth $50 to you, because they are not ample enough; but they are to me, there is the same amount of thought and rearrangement exhibited on them as if I had fully worked each plan out, and the rest would have been only mechanical labour for which the remaining sum of $50 would well have paid me.

Such an argument—that an architect sold his ideas, not his drawings—loomed large in the struggle for professional status in the middle of the nineteenth century.

THE HENRY BOODY HOUSE

Wheeler's other known commission in Brunswick is the house for Professor Henry Hill Boody, a teacher of Greek and Rhetoric. It still stands across from the College and has been on the National Register of Historic Places since 1975.[24] Wheeler's first known executed commission in this country, it is among the best known of his designs today.

The house is usually dated 1848–49.[25] There is a full set of 12 large signed, undated, ruled ink-and-wash drawings on Whatman paper for the house in the College archives that range from site plan to full-size details of interior moldings (Figures 2–4).

They are remarkably dry for a colorist, but they demonstrate that Wheeler reached this country fully formed as draftsman and builder. Illustrations of works based on the house appeared in several publications, often with long descriptions, including *The Horticulturalist* for August 1849 (there designated "An English Cottage"), A. J. Downing's *Architecture of Country Houses* (as a

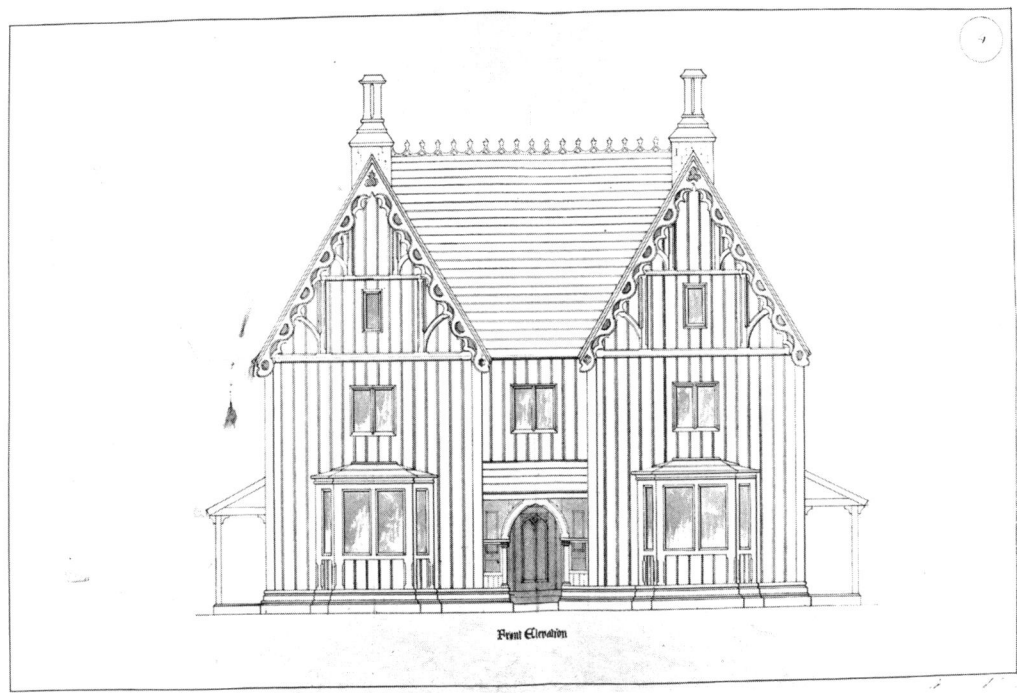

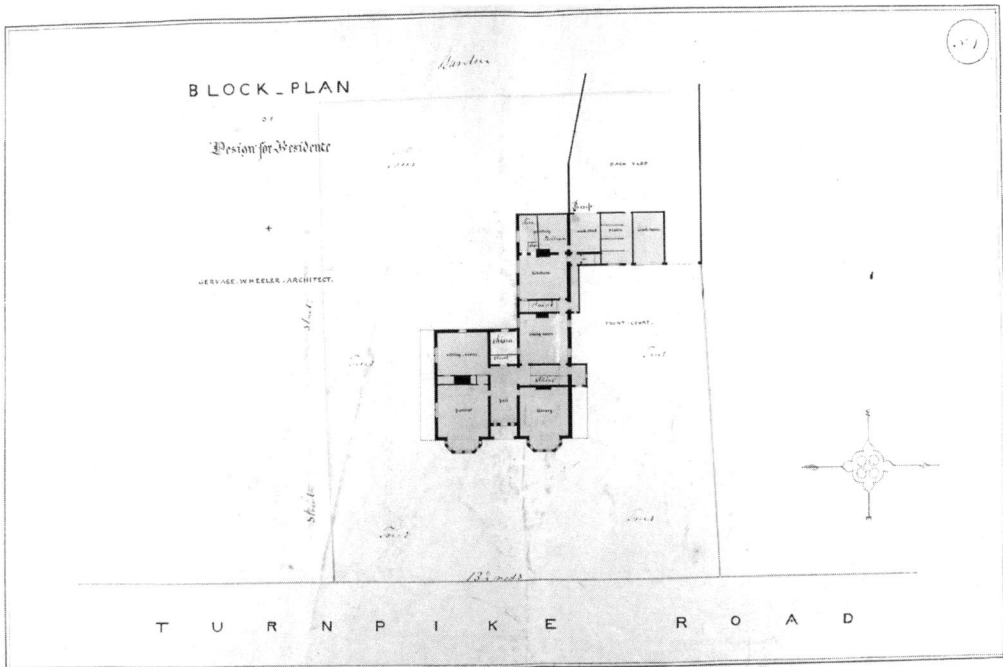

Figure 2. (top) *Gervase Wheeler, Drawing of the front elevation of the Henry Hill Boody House, Brunswick, Maine. (Courtesy Bowdoin College Archives, Brunswick, Maine.)*

Figure 3. (bottom) *Gervase Wheeler, Drawing of the block plan, Boody House. (Courtesy Bowdoin College Archives, Brunswick, Maine.)*

Figure 4. *Gervase Wheeler, Drawing of interior details, Boody House. (Courtesy Bowdoin College Archives, Brunswick, Maine.)*

Figure 5.
"Plain Timber Cottage-Villa" (a version of the Boody House).
(From Downing, The Architecture of Country Houses, *1850.)*

Figure 6.
*Boody House.
(O'Gorman photo,
2008.)*

"Plain Timber Cottage-Villa") (Figure 5), and *Appleton's Cyclopaedia of Drawing* of 1857.[26]

These invariably show chimneys (and thus fireplaces) moved inward, necessitating changes in the plan; barge boards that differ from the original; third-story windows in the gables; and the north porch removed. As modified it became the residence of Benjamin Butman in Worcester, Massachusetts, and appeared in William Brown's *The Carpenter's Assistant* as revised by Lewis Joy in 1853.[27] Other nineteenth-century reflections of the design stand in Canandaigua, New York, and elsewhere.[28] More recently, in the 1970s, drawings of the house were reproduced by Architectural Period Houses Inc., as one in a series of contemporary adaptations of period designs.[29] With this, among the earliest of his realized commissions, Wheeler's work gained broad recognition. It would happen more than once. Such continuing popularity attests to his ability to charm the American public with his domestic designs. His subsequent publications would follow suit.

The existing house shows that it was built with some variation from the drawings now at Bowdoin; it also has several important later additions. The most conspicuous of the latter is the entrance porch, which does not appear on the drawings and appears to have been constructed as late as the 1870s. The house is otherwise amazingly well preserved after 160 years. The double gables and steeply pitched roof emphasize the verticality of a design that is further enhanced by the upright board-and-batten siding (see Frontispiece; Figure 6). Ornamental barge boards enliven the gable ends.

But this was not some abstract proposition. Wheeler claimed to have formulated the scheme in response to the local constraints of materials and weather. The availability of wood meant that the Picturesque design, constructed in timber, would be "the result, as all architectural beauty must be, of fitness and harmony."[30] He placed the chimneys on the interior for optimal heat retention, and designed the drawing room and parlor suite, opening to verandas, to enable the closing off of one or the other. The floor plan was arranged in an irregular H shape, with a kitchen and service wing projecting at the rear. There, frontal symmetry gave way to flexible planning.

The Boody House represents a union of the Picturesque and Downingesque fitness to purpose. The house was designed to blend with its surroundings by virtue of material, varied massing, and asymmetrical plan—all hallmarks of the Picturesque. The honest expression of timber construction conformed to ideas of truth in architectural expression, a basic component of the architectural theory of the time.[31]

New Haven, Connecticut, 1847–1849

As we know, Wheeler had traveled in Connecticut in 1847. He there met Henry Austin, an architect of local renown in New Haven, and established an agreement to work with him in an arrangement that allowed him employment at Brunswick as well. Other than correspondence from Wheeler himself, however, there has been no documentation of a working relationship between the two architects. Austin is said to have apprenticed under Ithiel Town and started his own office in 1837. The work he produced during the half-century of his practice reflected the modes of the time and included commissions both public and residential. His practice peaked in the 1850s, so that his office was very much on the upswing when Wheeler worked with him.[1]

PROJECT FOR A COLLEGE CHAPEL, HARTFORD

In September 1847, Wheeler wrote to Leonard Woods of his collaboration with Austin for a project at Hartford: "They talk of erecting a college chapel there and Mr. Austin and myself are I suppose certain of doing it."[2] Perhaps Wheeler's training with Carpenter led to Austin's engaging him for this task. It seems, however, that the commission never materialized, as no chapel was erected at what became Trinity College during this period.[3] An understanding was apparently reached for some unspecified work "in connection with [the] organ at Trinity" that in 1850 was contracted to Austin. It is unclear, but doubtful, whether Wheeler, who by then was in Philadelphia, remained connected to that job, even though he had lived and worked in Hartford before moving on to Pennsylvania.

In addition to his association with Henry Austin, Wheeler may have hoped his acquaintance with the Reverend Woods would prove helpful in New Haven. In the same correspondence in which he mentioned the college chapel in Hartford (that is, in September 1847), he asked Woods's help in introducing him to the minister's peers in the New Haven and Hartford areas. He specifically requested "a few lines of introduction to Dr. Williams" as well as "amongst the professors" in New Haven.[4] Dr. John Williams had recently assumed the presidency of Trinity College. Like Woods, his background included several advanced degrees, travel in France and England, and teaching experience.

Correspondence during this phase of Wheeler's career helps us to understand his own aspirations and frustrations. With his background in English Ecclesiology,

[29]

it is not surprising to discover that he had hoped to work on church architecture. Through Reverend Woods, Wheeler sought connections in ecclesiastical and educational worlds. According to correspondence between Woods and Richard Upjohn, Wheeler was introduced not only to Dr. John Williams but to Dr. Croswell of the Church of the Advent in Boston, George Sumner, M.D., a professor of botany at Trinity College and vestryman of Christ Church in Hartford,[5] and the Rev. Andrew Dunning, a Bowdoin graduate and later minister of the Congregational church in Thompson, Connecticut.[6] There has been no evidence to suggest that any commissions resulted from these introductions. In fact, this correspondence postdates Wheeler's departure from Brunswick in 1848, and, as we shall see, Woods cited these clerics as people who would give negative assessments of the architect's reliability. Wheeler's few known ecclesiastical works came from other commissioners.

It was also at this time that Wheeler apparently hoped to establish contacts through Sir Charles Wesley in London. The letter from Wesley in August of 1848 is an obvious response to a plea from Wheeler for assistance: "I regret exceedingly," wrote Wesley, "that I have no personal acquaintance with any of the Bishops or Clergymen of the Episcopal Church in America or it would have given me sincere gratification to have served you in any way by such introductions . . . , but I will make every endeavor to procure you some amongst my clerical friends."[7] It would seem that nothing came of this.

Wheeler attempted to convince the Bowdoin College committee and Upjohn of the appropriateness of a more current mode of design for the Chapel. At that point he must have had great hopes of disseminating his firsthand knowledge of the recent innovations in church architecture and decoration associated with Pugin, Carpenter, and the Cambridge Camden Society. In a letter he denounced the design of one church that Austin's office was completing at the time as being "of a character that I am glad to have escaped any connection with." It can be inferred from this that Wheeler's views regarding the proper design of church architecture were firmly ingrained. The letter continues:

> It will be a long while before I dare attempt to introduce anything of the kind here and as it is, on the whole I am rather glad perhaps that there are no churches going on as I know I should be cruelly mortified in having to shape my ideas of propriety and beauty and correctness in accordance with those of the "critics" about me.[8]

Wheeler clearly considered neither the American public nor the architectural profession sophisticated enough to appreciate the more advanced designs of an architect with his background. He suspended his pursuit of Ecclesiological architecture only a year and a half after his arrival in the United States.

Figure 7.
*Gervase Wheeler for Henry Austin,
New Haven House, ca. 1848–50.
(The New Haven Museum and
Historical Society.)*

NEW HAVEN HOUSE HOTEL (FOR HENRY AUSTIN)

Wheeler wrote that he worked on one project while in Austin's office, a large hotel to be erected in New Haven. His own comments on the building suggest that what work he had previously accomplished was largely in the Picturesque modes of dwellings or the vocabulary of Gothic Revival. As he prepared the drawings for exhibit, he called them "rather an experiment on my part the style being very chaste and purely worked but Italian; one of the fronts being very like [Charles] Barry's Travelers Club House in London." The design might have been inspired by Barry's Italian Renaissance–based work, but it was hardly "very like" it.

The commission was in all likelihood the New Haven House, now demolished, on the Green at the corner of Chapel and College Streets, a building credited to Austin's office.[9] Erected in 1850, it was a large, foursquare Renaissance Revival block whose main façade on the Green was six bays wide and reached five stories plus attic in height (Figure 7). It is not clear whether Wheeler designed the

Figure 8.
Gervase Wheeler, Project for an Italian villa, ca. 1848–49. (Historic New England.)

structure or was only the draftsman, although the crisply detailed building stood out from other more ornamental work that came from the Austin office about the same time. If Wheeler did design it, it would represent one of the few public buildings attributed to him, later assertions to the contrary. The introductory comments to an article written by Wheeler that appeared in 1851 in *The Home Journal*, a weekly paper published in New York City, noted that "though he has been eminently successful in the large public buildings he has designed and erected, yet rural architecture is his preference."[10] His preference, or his lot?

PROJECT FOR AN ITALIAN VILLA

Historic New England in Boston owns a set of drawings by Wheeler for an Italian villa that probably fits into this period. There is no date, place, and client given on the sheets. The first floor plan is not signed; the elevations are.[11] The drawings entered the Boston collection with others from Henry Austin's office, suggesting a date around 1848–49. It is a rudimentary design compared to Wheeler's later projects in this mode. The plan combines a rectangular central-hall block with asymmetrical extensions for a tower and service wing. The elevations show a broad, two-story, hip-roofed residence of boxy shapes with trabeated and half-round arched windows whose frames are akin to those used by Austin, wrap-around veranda, and three-story campanile with half-round arched windows in the belvedere (Figure 8). The exterior was to be composed of (flush?) horizontal boards over a lumber frame; the roof, standing metal seam. The whole lacks the richly Picturesque look of Wheeler's other Italian residences (or Austin's, for that matter), and may be an early exercise in the type.[12]

It is not possible to assess in detail the influence of Wheeler's own designs on Henry Austin's work or the converse.[13] At any rate, Wheeler's association with the New Haven architect lasted little more than 18 months, during which he spent time away in Brunswick. As was his wont, he expressed dissatisfaction with several works coming out of Austin's office. It would not be implausible to suggest that his condescending manner again led to uncomfortable relations and an early departure.

Hartford, Connecticut, 1849

After his year and a half in Austin's orbit, Wheeler must have felt confident enough of his reputation, or perhaps sufficiently frustrated with the interpretation and execution of modes in that office, to establish his own practice. He had moved to Hartford by April 1849. With his residence at the American House, he opened an office in Janes's Buildings on Main Street.[1] Ironically, though only sparse documentation as to his stay in Hartford exists, we have it on his authority that this was among the busiest periods of his career. In June, Wheeler wrote to Upjohn to ask for his assistance in procuring a draftsman.[2] Relations between the two men at this point are difficult to assess. Although Upjohn was surely tired of Wheeler's interference in Brunswick, he had recently answered a letter from Wheeler with a "kind reply," and Wheeler thanked him "for the good wishes contained in the concluding portion of . . . [your] letter which I sincerely appreciate." Those good wishes, assuming they were real, would be taxed shortly. Upjohn had earlier referred Wheeler to a Mr. Jordan, who entered Wheeler's office on a temporary engagement. With business "steadily increasing," Wheeler found himself in need of permanent help. Two young men in his employ, apparently qualified only as copyists, could not meet the exigencies of the position of design assistant. Wheeler required someone he could rely upon to develop designs from his sketches; he was sufficiently busy and "called away so much that I can hardly settle down to anything myself in the way of drawing." His known output during this time ranged from the publication of drawings to actual commissions, and one literary endeavor.

The earliest known example of Wheeler's written work appeared in a book for students of graphic art published in Hartford early in 1849. Entitled *The Columbian Drawing Book*, this volume, compiled by Charles Conrad Kuchel, comprises a series of lithographic copies of drawings by various artists with accompanying written "directions for the assistance of the student." None of the plates is signed by Wheeler; the eloquent directions were his contribution to the work. The closing sentence evokes the pleasure and fulfillment to be derived by the student from the art of drawing:

> [L]et his eye, his heart, and his hand work together, and he will be repaid by the increased keenness of the one, the emotions of the other, and the skill of the third, for the time and thought he has bestowed.

The work was well received, with reviews in several journals, including *The Horticulturist* and *The Literary World*.³ In each case it was recommended as a useful tool for the amateur who wanted to learn the essentials of drawing. Wheeler's participation in the production may indicate a want of architectural commissions, and may have been in recognition of the benefits of self-promotion, even in a field peripheral to architecture. He wrote convincingly of his subject, in articulate and expressive prose. As his American career progressed, his ability to write would serve him well.

As we have seen, the year 1849 also saw the publication of two residential designs by Wheeler in A. J. Downing's journal *The Horticulturist*: in June, a design for a "Villa in the Tudor Style" (Figure 9), and in August, "An English Cottage" (after the Boody House in Brunswick).⁴ The date of each contribution, May 16 and April 2 respectively, suggests that Downing and Wheeler had established contact by the spring of that year. The business relationship between the two men would lead Wheeler to further opportunities for publication, but Downing, too, would eventually sour on the man.

The inclusion of Wheeler's work in a respected monthly magazine must have benefited his career. *The Horticulturist* had great appeal among country "gentlemen." Articles dealt mainly with plants and landscaping, but as Downing espoused the picturesque integration of home and grounds, the magazine also provided a forum for architectural design. A. J. Davis, architect of many residences in the romantic mode of the period, had already collaborated with Downing to supply plans and elevations. Downing's use of Wheeler's works suggests that he appreciated the latter's comfortable handling of the Picturesque. Grecian revival design still lingered in the hands of many architects, and the vocabulary of the Picturesque was only beginning to gain acceptance in America in the 1840s. At this point Downing may have seen in Wheeler a peer who could understand and express the formulations of the American Picturesque.

Of the two designs, the one based on the Boody House has already been mentioned. Downing himself evidently considered that work worthy of promotion, but a regular correspondent to *The Horticulturist*, a Mr. Jeffreys of New York, objected to the title and perhaps the design of the "English Cottage": "Are we never to have any American cottages? . . . Try it again Mr. Wheeler."⁵ Wheeler intended the other design, "a Villa in the Tudor Style," as a gentleman's country residence. He considered the house, with its irregular but harmonized massing executed in stone or brick, to be "peculiarly adapted to those localities where the scenery was rather sylvan than wild." The plan, reflected on the exterior, provides for large communicating drawing and dining rooms en suite, a small conservatory for plants, and a library.⁶

VILLA IN THE TUDOR STYLE.

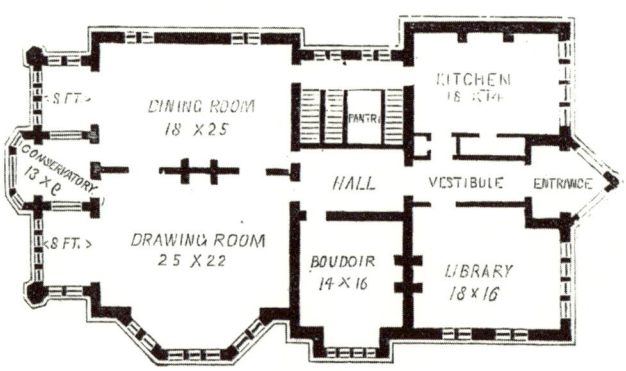

PRINCIPAL FLOOR.

Figure 9.
"Villa in the Tudor Style."
(From The Horticulturalist,
June 1849.)

Figure 10.
Olmstead House, East Hartford, Connecticut, 1849.
(From Rural Homes, *1851.)*

THE HENRY OLMSTEAD HOUSE, EAST HARTFORD, CONNECTICUT

The "Gothic" Olmstead House, erected "about a mile and a half from the village town of East Hartford," is one of two known executed domestic commissions to come from Wheeler's office during this year. He designed it for a member of a family prominent in the Hartford area. The plan, essentially cruciform, dictates the exterior massing of high intersecting gables. Constructed of wood and sheathed in vertical board and batten, "no ornamental work is any where introduced which does not serve some constructive purpose of design. . . . The bold projections of the roofs, posts, and tracery . . . [cast] interlacing lines of shadow that vary the [deep cream] tint most beautifully."[7] Like the Boody House, the Olmstead House combines in no uncertain terms the qualities of the Picturesque and its principle of honesty: a varied silhouette, extension of the house into the surrounding landscape through verandas, and rational construction (Figures 10, 11). The design has been the subject of study by Vincent Scully, who wrote that it "reinforced with a new and more incisive logic the practical and aesthetic principles of Downing's cottage style."[8] The house reportedly stands, though altered beyond recognition.

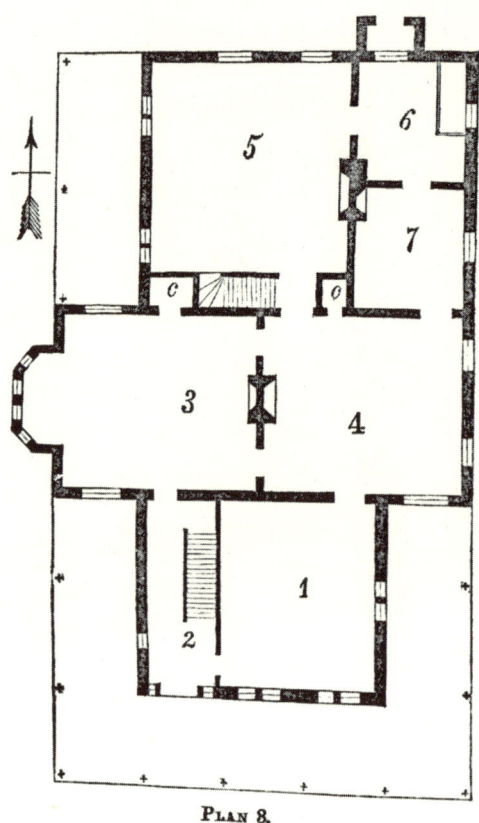

Figure 11.
Plan of the Olmstead House.
(*From* Rural Homes, *1851.*)

Figure 12.
After Gervase Wheeler, "The Willows," the Joseph Warren Revere House, Morristown, N.J., 1854 (From the Collection of the Morris County Park Commission.)

Wheeler published the design in *Rural Homes* two years after its erection. It would provide the model for "The Willows," the house built in Morristown, New Jersey, in 1854 for Joseph Warren Revere (Figure 12). The Willows is now listed on the New Jersey State Register as well as the National Register of Historic Places. Its plan, elevation, and architectural details follow those of the Olmstead House very closely. Modifications include the opening of the front stair hall, enlargement of the dining room and parlor, and addition of a rear stair and kitchen ell. Wheeler was practicing in New York at the time that Revere began The Willows, but we have not discovered documents linking the architect and the client, or proving that Wheeler had an active role in the adapted design.[9]

ROCKWOOD, THE EDWIN BARTLETT RESIDENCE, NORTH TARRYTOWN, NEW YORK

The modest Olmstead House was designed to harmonize with its surroundings; Rockwood, an imposing stone villa, sat prominently atop a hill overlooking the Hudson River.[10] The owner, successful importer and merchant Edwin Bartlett, gathered several hundred acres to form his estate and commissioned Wheeler to design the residence in 1849. As is often the case, we have no information about how the architect, still in his mid-twenties, was selected to design such an imposing structure, or how the two men met, but the commission for such a grand house after just two years in America was an impressive achievement.

The asymmetrical scheme rose in the castellated Gothic mode expressed in grey gneiss (Figure 13). A four-story corner tower rising above the living room dominated the 140-foot front façade. The tower was balanced across an arched carriage porch by an advancing two-and-a-half-story octagonal bay. The major living spaces opened onto verandas with fine views of the Hudson. The interior finishes included walnut and oak paneling and a richly carved stair balustrade with Gothic motifs.

The house appeared in a sketch by Edwin Whitefield, an itinerant artist who solicited patrons door-to-door in the early 1850s. In his rendering of a neighboring estate, the profile of Rockwood's tower rises clearly over the trees on the hillside.[11] From the start Wheeler's design received critical acclaim from popular journals and authors. An 1856 issue of *The Horticulturist* featured Rockwood in a column entitled "Visits to Country Places" which described it as a "princely mansion."[12] Henry Sargent, editor of the sixth edition of Downing's *Theory and Practice of Landscape Gardening*, lauded it again, calling it "the most marked place which has been created since the first edition of this book."[13] An 1860 pictorial essay

Figure 13.
*Rockwood, the Edward Bartlett Residence, North Tarrytown, New York, 1849.
(From John Zukowsky,* Hudson River Houses.*)*

on the finer residences along the Hudson opened with two photolithographs of the place.[14]

In the same year *Knickerbocker Magazine* ran two articles on "The Hudson." Essentially a descriptive history of the landscapes and legends of the area, a few homes were highlighted: Sunnyside, the residence of Washington Irving, and "the beautiful chateau of Rockwood."[15] The design withstood the vagaries of taste, as it again appeared among the outstanding homes of America listed by Martha Lamb in 1878 as "not only a fine specimen of mechanical skill, but a work of art and architectural propriety. . . . [it] challenges comparison with the best homes of any country."[16] Wheeler had again achieved a publicity coup, although by the date of this article he was no longer around to profit from it.

The enduring popular appeal of Rockwood for some thirty years after its construction testified to the facility of the architect. The estate changed hands only three times, and in the late 1880s, the new owner, William Rockefeller, nearly doubled it in size. In 1922, three years after Rockefeller's death, the once "princely mansion" was destroyed. Only the gatehouse on the Albany Post Road remained.[17]

Wheeler was especially proud of Rockwood; he displayed drawings of it in

Figure 14.
Congregational Church, Berlin, Conn., 1849–50, as it exists today.
(O'Gorman photo, 2009.)

Figure 15.
R. C. Carpenter, St. Paul's, Brighton, 1846–48.
(From The Ecclesiologist, *June, 1846.)*

an exhibition at the Pennsylvania Academy of the Fine Arts in Philadelphia the year after designing it,[18] and would include some aspect of it in his two American books. He never published an elevation, however, perhaps in deference to his client's privacy.

CONGREGATIONAL CHURCH, BERLIN, CONNECTICUT

Wheeler executed at least one ecclesiastical commission during his Hartford stay. On the first of November 1849, the New Haven *Register* carried a solicitation from his Janes's Buildings office of "tenders for [the] erection of a Wooden Church in the Gothic style" for the Berlin Congregationalists. The design as erected is not easy to reconstruct; apparently no original drawings survive and the building has been reworked many times (see Figure 14). Either badly designed or badly built or both, it required repairs immediately and continuously throughout its life. The original steeple was "deemed out of proportion," according to the official history of the church, so in 1863 it was sheathed in another, higher one, ironically enough designed by Henry Austin.[19] Precisely what remains of Wheeler's interior is yet to be determined, but despite its pointed openings, as a whole the building follows traditional New England religious architecture: a preaching hall with galleries beneath a broad gable, and a tower and steeple centered on the main axis. Such an ecclesiastical design scarcely reflected his training with Carpenter (see Figure 15), or, since it is close in type to Henry Austin's contemporary wooden churches, hardly justifies his haughty distain for that architect's work of the same period. Although his later church at Owego, New York, and the chapel at Williams College proved to be more satisfactory designs, Wheeler seems to have been wise to concentrate on rural domestic design, which was well received as erected or published in his popular books.

Philadelphia, Pennsylvania, 1849–1850

Although he gave the impression of enjoying a healthy practice in Hartford, we soon find Wheeler seeking work in Philadelphia. A business flyer printed for him in the city gives his address as 70 Walnut Street (in the American Fire Insurance Company building, just down from the Insurance Company of North America which he was to design), and "respectfully offers his services to those contemplating building" (see Figure 45). As references it lists prominent locals, C. H. [sic] Fisher, Harry Ingersoll,[1] and Benjamin Gerard, a prominent lawyer and trustee of the University of Pennsylvania, all of Philadelphia, and A. I. [sic] Downing of Newburgh, New York.[2] Such a printed flyer suggests that he hoped to stay in the area for a while.

BROOKWOOD, THE HENRY C. FISHER HOUSE

Wheeler's contributions to A. J. Downing's *The Horticulturist* may have resulted in direct contact with the editor, although there is only circumstantial evidence to support this. At the end of 1849 Downing sponsored Wheeler on a trip to Philadelphia, where Downing had earlier come to consult with Henry C. Fisher about his new estate. In December, Wheeler presented himself to Fisher with a letter of introduction from Downing.[3]

Fisher had recently purchased fifty acres of land in the countryside to the north of Philadelphia and wanted a comfortable and luxurious estate. With the help of Downing, he had chosen a site for his home and a landscaping plan; all that remained was to design the house itself. Fisher and Wheeler first met at dinner on 12 December 1849. By 23 December the architect had submitted two designs for Fisher's inspection, one Italianate, the other Elizabethan. Sidney Fisher, a close relative, wrote in his diary: "the latter is not only in itself the handsomer by far, in my judgment, but accords well with the picturesque character of the surrounding scenery."[4] The Elizabethan was apparently the design adopted. As the construction of Brookwood progressed over the next two years, it was invariably described as elegant, convenient, and luxurious.[5]

Much as had been the case with Rockwood, Brookwood received applause for its thoroughly considered plan and pleasant aspect. In the appendix to the sixth edition of Downing's *Landscape Gardening*, after the sketch of Rockwood, a brief entry calls Brookwood a "very extensive and complete establishment" sure

Figure 16.
"An American Country House of the First Class."
Perhaps Brookwood, the Henry C. Fisher House, Philadelphia, 1849–50.
(From A. J. Downing, The Architecture of Country Houses.*)*

to become "one of the most striking places near Philadelphia."[6] The building was demolished in the 1960s, and no photographs have as yet been uncovered. There is reason to speculate, however, that Wheeler's design for the Fisher estate was published by Downing.

Downing's *Architecture of Country Houses* appeared in 1850. In it, the author featured two designs by "Gervase Wheeler, Esq., of Philadelphia, an architect of reputation."[7] By introducing Wheeler in his book, as he had done in his magazine, Downing expressed his respect for the architect and complimented the designs for their "artistic ability, combined with an excellent knowledge of all that belongs to domestic life in its best development."

The first design, numbered XXV, "A Plain Timber Cottage-Villa," was a slightly modified version of the Henry Boody house erected in Brunswick, already familiar to the reader. The second design, numbered XXX, "An American Country House of the First Class," was prepared specifically for the book, according to Downing (Figure 16). Wheeler's usual thorough explanation accompanied the illustrations.[8] The architect considered the "Large Country House," as the design is alternately labeled, a simple work, catering to the gentleman of average means.

The mode of expression, he wrote, "without being a copy of any of one of the well-known Tudor or Elizabethan types, has as distinct a character as they have." In a scheme similar though less elaborate than Rockwood, the configuration of the plan balances the main living quarters with the kitchen and service wing on either side of a carriage porch and entrance hall. The library, drawing room, and dining room open onto verandas and thus to the grounds. Wheeler suggested that the interior decor be simple, but continued with a prescription for stained glass for the windows of the halls, staircase, and library.

The Architecture of Country Houses appeared at approximately the same time as Henry Fisher began to build Brookwood. The descriptive text accompanying design XXX does not mention an actual commission, but it is possible that this was the project proposed to Fisher. Both designs were Elizabethan in style. A comparison of the floor plan of the "Large Country House" with the footprint of the Fisher residence from period insurance survey atlases shows the same general configuration, with a two-and-a-half-story main block and a service wing projecting off the right of the main entrance. In the atlases the placement of verandas is expanded, but this may have occurred naturally over time.[9] The type of residence, a country home for a gentleman, was the same in each case. And it should be remembered that the design would have been submitted for publication some time prior to the printed date of the volume, thereby allowing for the lack of information as to actual construction. Then, too, Fisher may not have wanted his name published.

A MISSED OPPORTUNITY:
THE PHILADELPHIA COUNTY COURT BUILDING

The meeting between Wheeler and the Fishers led to an introduction that, had the timing been different, might have provided Wheeler with an opportunity to work on a large prominently placed public commission. Among the other guests Sidney Fisher invited to dinner on 12 December 1849 was Benjamin Gerard, one of the men Wheeler had mentioned as references on his advertising flyer, and a member of the Select and Common Councils of Philadelphia. The purpose of the introduction, Fisher stated, was to afford Wheeler "a chance of competing for the buildings about to be erected by the County for Courts, etc., on Independence Square."[10]

In 1849 the Common and Select Councils sought design submissions for a new courthouse. On 5 December the county solicitor forwarded a letter requesting approval of erection of a new courthouse and enclosing proposals and estimates from three local architects: John Haviland, Thomas U. Walter, and Napoleon

Lebrun.[11] Fifteen days later, the Select and Common Councils resolved that a county courthouse could be built at the corner of Sixth and Walnut Streets on State House Square, provided architectural plans were approved. The resolution drew continued controversy, and by 27 June 1850, the building committee of the Common Council had rescinded the resolution of the previous December.[12] It was not until April 1866 that a site was selected on Sixth below Chestnut and the Common Council initiated the erection of a courthouse, which was completed in February 1867. At no point do the journals and ledgers mention Wheeler. With the submission on 5 December of the various proposals, Fisher's introduction to Gerard may have been too late to benefit him other than as a reference.

THE INSURANCE COMPANY OF NORTH AMERICA

After completion of the designs for Brookwood, Wheeler was not without occupation in Philadelphia. The Insurance Company of North America had simultaneously resolved to erect a new office headquarters, and a committee of three was appointed on 14 January 1850 to find an acceptable plan. By 26 February Wheeler had been chosen for the job. The method of selecting an architect was not discussed in company documents, and a survey of names of the corporate directors did not immediately suggest a contact for Wheeler. However, Wheeler drew the plans and received $75 for services rendered.[13] He offered to superintend the construction of the building, but Abraham Masson was awarded the building contract. Upon its completion in December 1850 the company minutes called it a "beautifully appropriate building." A history of the company published in 1885 included an engraving of the façade as it appeared in 1879 (Figure 17).[14]

The masonry building rose as a three-bay, three-story configuration with an eclectic use of motifs. A broad flat set of steps, the entire width of the office, led customers up to the entrance. Above the first floor architrave,[15] more classically detailed piers supported the round-arched arcade of windows with Gothic tracery. The third-floor openings were squared off, and though repeating the tracery, had much flatter frames and reveals. A curved gable centered over the middle bay added still more variety to the line of the bracketed roof cornice. The structure was demolished in August 1880, together with the adjoining Farquar Building to the east, in order to make space for more commodious offices designed by Cabot and Chandler of Boston.

Figure 17.
Insurance Company of North America, Philadelphia, 1850 (on the right).
(*From* A History of the Insurance Company of North America, 1885.)

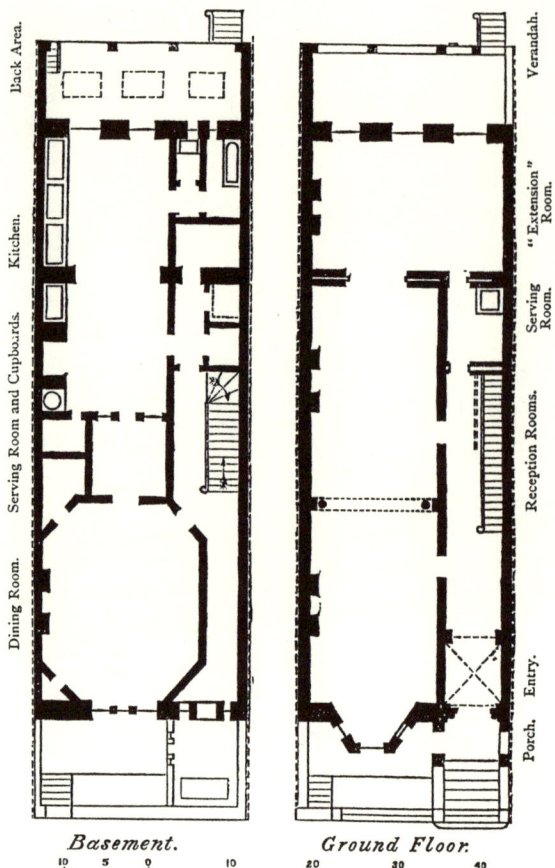

Figure 18.
Plans of an unnamed Philadelphia townhouse, ca. 1850.
(*From* The Choice of a Dwelling.)

UNNAMED TOWNHOUSE

Another project apparently undertaken at this time, but for which there is almost no information, was the design of a townhouse. The only known reference to it occurs in Wheeler's *The Choice of a Dwelling*, published in England in 1871.[16] He shows basement and ground floor plans of a typical narrow townhouse with side hall configuration (Figure 18). Kitchen and octagonal dining room occupy the raised basement, double parlors divided by an arch and a tearoom take up most of the elevated ground level, and there are chambers above. The address, date, and client are not listed, and further documentation has not emerged.[17]

New York City, 1850–1851

By late February 1851 Wheeler had returned to New York.[1] Waiting for more permanent office space, he rented rooms at 304 West Fourteenth Street; by May he was listed in the city directory as "Architect, University, Washington Square."[2] As he had in Hartford, Wheeler recognized the advertising possibilities of listing in an urban directory. In a letter written on 17 March, he again appealed to Richard Upjohn, this time for potential odd jobs, but only until May, the date of publication of the directory.[3] And he must have recognized, too, that an office in the Gothic Revival New York University building designed in the 1830s by Ithiel Town and James Dakin, where A. J. Davis and other designers also lived and worked, would set the right tone.

Wheeler began immediately to make his presence known. His letter to Upjohn announced his new location, and again asked for help. Our understanding of the relationship between the two men remains somewhat unresolved. During the project at Bowdoin, Wheeler had antagonized Upjohn and a great deal of tension had resulted. Still, the contact was established, and in apparent recognition of Upjohn's influence, Wheeler now returned to him, "remembering the unvarying kindness you have always shown in speaking of me." He offered his services and expertise for any commissions that Upjohn might be unable to fulfill: "if at any time you . . . have work you cannot from press of business undertake [I] shall be very happy to have it placed in my hands and will do my best." Wheeler went on to claim that his practice had thrived in the years since the Bowdoin Chapel episode: "Since I last saw you, I have done a great deal in various parts of the country and very successfully." The accuracy of Wheeler's assurance may have been slanted by the tendency toward exaggeration we have previously witnessed, and perhaps a bit of self-deception. He had indeed seen a number of buildings rise from his drawings, but an ongoing successful and busy practice would hardly require him to seek work from others. And an architect would be inclined to hand over only commissions in inconvenient locations, with difficult clients, or which presented no particular design challenge or monetary gain.

On the other hand, Wheeler's peripatetic existence could explain his need for contacts in New York. Having worked first in Maine, then Connecticut, and most recently Philadelphia, whatever reputation he had established did not necessarily follow him to New York. Letters of introduction, recommendations, or regular correspondence would then have formed the basis for the development of a new clientele in the new area, but we know of no such documents. Under the circumstances the most natural response for Wheeler was to turn to previous contacts such as Upjohn for assistance and references. But as we shall see, in this case it proved ultimately not to be a wise move.

Of particular importance in Wheeler's practice were his published writings. He contributed essays to periodicals, foremost among them *The Home Journal*, and published his own books. On the first of March 1851, a series of sixteen articles written by him (presumably initiated in Philadelphia or perhaps even in Hartford) began to appear in the *Journal*, a popular weekly magazine described by its editors, Nathaniel Parker Willis and George Morris, as a chronicle of fashion, society, theater, and the arts, leaving "the details of politics and heavier matters to the daily newspapers."[4] As in most journals of the period, contributors were seldom paid for their pieces, and articles were often printed anonymously.[5] But *The Home Journal* was considered somewhat more sophisticated than its competitors, with writing that often approached the level of literature.

The details of Wheeler's association with the editors of *The Home Journal* remain purely conjectural. Nathanial Willis, who sought out new contributors to maintain a fresh magazine, may have met the architect in person and encouraged him to submit a series of articles. Or perhaps Wheeler took the initiative. It seems that, with the exception of the introduction to the *Columbian Drawing Book* and the submissions to *The Horticulturist* in 1849, this was the beginning of Wheeler's career as a writer. While the articles were not signed, the appearance of the initials "G.W." may have been enough to distinguish Wheeler from other architects practicing in New York. This subtle means of identification may have made future commissions possible.

The articles for the most part belonged to a multipart feature entitled "On Perfecting a Home."[6] The editors introduced the series with enthusiasm and confidence, promoted its author as "an eminent and practical architect," and "emphatically commend[ed] our correspondent and his views to the reader's attention." Although a pitch for Wheeler, the compliment also promoted the journal itself. Years later, when reviewing Wheeler's *Homes for the People* of 1855, the editors would "claim an interest" in the success of the architect as a result of having earlier provided their periodical as a forum for his views.[7]

"On Perfecting a Home" addressed the definition of fitness and the realization of comfort in the American residence. The first article in the series, entitled "Home, How to Build One Cheaply and Well," began by distinguishing a house from a home. The latter, Wheeler asserted, was different: because it suited to the client, and because it used the skills and abilities of a professional architect. As usual, a self-promotional tone prevailed. Wheeler, having defined the need for "practical statements, easily understood directions, evident reasons, [and] common sense determinations," proceeded to provide them. The basic considerations in building any house included "convenient arrangement, facility of construction and of repair, perfect protection from heat and cold, adequate means of warming and ventilating, congruity with the scenery around." Period styles take a back seat in this formulation. These introductory points provided the outline for the series.

Choice of site occupied the first article. It was to be derived from considerations of shelter, shade, access to water, and views, not distant, but of "the familiar objects near the eye that are varying ever." The arrangement of a residence depended specifically on the compass orientation of rooms for maximum comfort and convenience, not unlike a "tech-built" house of the post–World War II period. The kitchen, for instance, belonged at the north side, "leaving more desirable points of the compass for the main building." If the family ate the main meal of the household at midday, for best natural lighting the dining room should open to the east; if at evening, it should open to the west. North was to be avoided for the entrance because of the threat of penetrating cold and wind; the southern exposure was reserved for the most often used room, the parlor or salon. From the point of view of fitness, Wheeler considered that the rural or suburban house required no formal parlor, for it would be "too party-ish and pretentious for the country."

Each article, or grouping when the subject necessitated it, tackled a particular topic, such as building to suit the landscape, materials and their treatment in construction, ventilation and heating, outbuildings, furniture, and examples of residential types. Wheeler described several designs, the "Modern Italian Bracketed Style," "Summer Lodge," "Suburban Villa," and "Southern Home." Concerns paralleling the Picturesque point of view and the theories of Downing permeate the articles. Full consideration of the house within the landscape meant that "the building and the grounds, the natural objects and the result of art, are in perfect congruity" achieving "home beauty" (April 19). And "a home in the sunny south is a very different thing to arrange to one suited to a northern clime" (July 5).[8]

In addition to the series "On Perfecting a Home," Wheeler submitted an article that, though not directly related to architecture, once more contained a subtle form of self-promotion. "The Hudson and the Rhine" (June 14) had nothing to do with the Rhine other than using it to raise romantic associations. Wheeler, who was at this time or soon thereafter to design several houses for the area, described the beauty of the Hudson River Valley and the numerous ideal locations for country dwellings. Although again the piece was signed simply "G.W.," by this time regular readers would have been familiar with the identity of the author. (A similar article, "Upstream," by G. W., appeared a few years later, on 2 June 1855. It coincided with the publication of Wheeler's second book, and shared the pages of *The Home Journal* with a review of that volume. Once again, the subject matter was the Hudson River Valley, and the article linked constructing a country home and hiring an architect like Wheeler to design it.)

The continuing editorial comments that accompanied Wheeler's articles in *The Home Journal* indicate that the pieces were favorably received. With the second article in the 8 March issue, the editors noted that "we find that we responded to a want of the Public Mind, by introducing our writer." A month later, the article of 12 April opened with the following tribute: "his ideas have been so suited to the Public Want, that most of them, as they have appeared, have taken shape in the plans of projected houses in the country." The basis for these statements is never clear; nevertheless, the continuation of the series does suggest its popular appeal.

The success of the series emboldened Wheeler to publish it as a book. At the end of his article describing an Entrance Lodge (24 May), Wheeler wrote that, "urged by many friends, I have enlarged upon the topics that have now connected me with the readers of *The Home Journal* more than three months, and shall shortly publish a volume upon 'Rural Homes.'" He had already chosen the title, and the resulting work, *Rural Homes; or Sketches of Houses Suited to American Country Life, with Original Plans, Designs, &c.*, signed in full on the title page but with just the initials "G. W." at the preface, appeared later that year as an illustrated duodecimo volume from the distinguished publishing house of Charles Scribner in New York.

Comparison of the two groups of materials shows that the book essentially elaborated on the articles. Wheeler repeated many of them verbatim or with minor transposition of paragraphs, and refined, edited, or expanded others. For example, chapter 2, "General Arrangement of a House Upon the Ground," corresponds to the second article in the series, but includes a disclaimer to the effect that Wheeler's designs were "not for actual embodiment and execution," but to serve as models that an architect might translate for the client. If they were copied he would lose a fee. In another instance, the depiction of "A Suburban Villa,"[9] (Figure 19), the author changed the tense from article to book, implying that the house had been erected in the interim between publication of the two formats.

Wheeler also added several chapters and sections to make *Rural Homes* more substantial than *The Home Journal* series. These included descriptions of "The Homestead," "The Parsonage House," "Cottages" (Figure 20), "Means of Artificial Warming," "Practical Directions to Amateurs Before Proceeding to Build," "Rural Architecture as a Fine Art," and addenda to three other chapters. In introducing the book, Wheeler indicated his intention to present, in organized fashion, considerations in the choice and construction of a country home which his audience might find useful. He stated, "I claim no title to originality," recognizing

Figure 19.
"Suburban Villa."
(From Rural Homes, *1851.)*

Figure 20.
"Small Cottage"
with rustic porch posts.
(From Rural Homes, *1851.)*

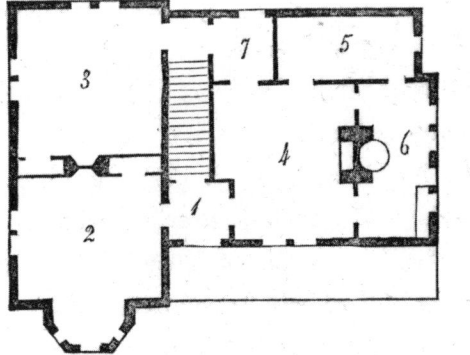

perhaps his debt to the English Picturesque and the precedence of A. J. Downing's influential publications.

In the final chapter on "Rural Architecture as a Fine Art" Wheeler produced a rambling paean to country living and a plea for its appropriate architectural expression. He cites the village of Grand-Pré in Longfellow's *Evangeline* (1847) as the perfect model. Set amid fields and meadows, "There in the tranquil evenings of summer, . . . brightly the sunset / Lighted the village street, and gilded the vanes on the chimneys" of houses "strongly built . . . with frames of oak and of chestnut. . . . / Thatched were the roofs, with dormer-windows; and gables projecting / Over the basement below protected and shaded the doorway." Constructive skills in building and mechanical contrivances are the "grand distinctions" of the age, he wrote; what was lacking was the *art* of architecture, the true principles of design. Modern adaptations of historical monuments pale before the originals. He looks for hope in rural architecture, which, if done well, will elevate society. Architectural beauty in a rural house depends on "simplicity, reality and intention." To this end he advocates, among other things, architectural education to replace the evolution of carpenter into designer that had produced by his day the "archy-tect" whom he scorned. This remains a too-little-known statement of architectural intent of the 1850s in America, the view from the outside by a well-versed immigrant.

Rural Homes was well received by the press.[10] Of the many known reviews, only two voiced negative comments. The notices appeared in popular journals such as *Harper's New Monthly Magazine* and *Godey's Lady's Book*; in somewhat more literary publications such as the *American Whig Review* and the *Literary World*; and in gardening and country magazines such as the *Genessee Farmer*, *Debow's Review*,[11] and *The Horticulturist*. An ad for the book in *The Genessee Farmer* quoted from reviews in religious publications (*Philadelphia Presbyterian* and *Hartford Religious Herald*), and daily newspapers (*New York Evening Mirror* and the *Albany Spectator*).[12] Such widespread notice demonstrates the broad popular appeal of Wheeler's literary presence on the American architectural scene of the 1850s.

In every case the reviewers applauded the usefulness of the volume and the practical, comprehensive information it contained. An enthusiasm for the quality and clarity of the presentation of material and the attractive, flowing style pervaded even the negative assessments. The *American Whig Review* opened its critique with the following representative commentary: "This is not only elegantly written, but an exceedingly sensible book. . . . Within a short compass, Mr. Wheeler has gracefully sketched off what may be done to reconcile and realize the highest demands of taste, comfort and elegance, even with moderate means."[13] *The Genessee Farmer* concluded that "the pleasure and instruction we

Figure 21.
"Southern Home."
(From Rural Homes, 1851.)

have derived makes us feel grateful to the author, and bespeak for his book a place in the library of every intelligent person who ever expects to build or improve a suburban, village, or country house."[14] In August of that year, in response to a reader's inquiry for good references on rural domestic architecture, landscaping, and fruit gardening, the editor of *The Genessee Farmer* suggested "three good works . . . Downing's *Landscape Gardening*, Wheeler's *Rural Homes*, [and] Barry's *Fruit Garden*."[15]

Negative reviews did appear. One, published in *Sartain's Magazine* in Philadelphia, though recognizing *Rural Homes* to be an "intelligent work" in "straight forward, intelligible" language, criticized the author for being "unfortunately deficient in fine artistic taste," with the exception of the "unquestionable elegance in effect" of a design for a "Southern Home"[16] (Figure 21).

Uncomplimentary comments in the pages of *The Horticulturist* came, surprisingly, from A. J. Downing, who but a year earlier had been promoting Wheeler.[17] Downing, now generally recognized as the leading authority on American Picturesque domestic architecture, took exception to Wheeler's description of his designs as "suited to American Country Life." Downing specifically attacked the frontispiece of *Rural Homes*, a composition called "The Homestead," and its designer: "how transparent is the fiction which covers Mr. Wheeler's English education," he wrote (Figure 22). Calling the design of the building a bastard style of Elizabethan, he exclaimed "Oh Mr. Wheeler! this may be sweetly pretty and it may be built for twelve thousand, but it is not a house suited to the American

Figure 22.
"The Homestead."
(Frontispiece to Rural Homes, *1851.)*

climate." This review's blatant *ad hominem* attack on Wheeler came in a discussion of the influence of foreign architects in America. Downing lumped Wheeler with the "pseudo-architects from abroad, who leave home with too small a smattering of professional knowledge to ensure success at home, and after three or four years of practice in this country . . . undertake to *direct* the popular taste." Although couched in general terms, what makes this seem so personal is the fact that Downing had just taken into partnership Calvert Vaux, a 26-year-old immigrant English architect whom he had met abroad in 1850.[18]

What also made Downing's generally harsh critique particularly noteworthy was the prior rapport the two men had shared. As we have seen, Downing earlier supported and published Wheeler's work. He had from the outset recognized the English tradition inherent in Wheeler's designs and views, and commended them for their distinctiveness. In this same context, it is ironic that a review of Downing's *Architecture of Country Houses* in the *Literary World*, though lauding the work as invaluable to those considering building, criticized it for its inability to present an American style of country architecture in lieu of modified European styles![19]

Downing's scathing remarks may have been in part a reaction to the competition presented by Wheeler's book. Earlier American architectural publications had addressed builders, giving them "a measurable degree of sophistication"[20] in the use of Roman or Greek classical details. With the domestically sized books of Downing and Wheeler, the usable forms of the past proliferated to accommodate the newly fashionable Picturesque styles, and the intended readership expanded to prospective homeowners who dreamed of building or who intended to build. The competition was for the attention of the new audience. According to *The Literary World*, *Rural Homes* was "of less bulk and cost than Mr. Downing's book," *The Architecture of Country Houses* of 1850, "but contains much that is valuable on the subject."[21] In other words, Wheeler's work provided much the same sort of information for the general reader and was more accessible. An 1853 list of best-selling books, however, makes clear that Downing's publications sold in the thousands while Wheeler's *Rural Homes* is unmentioned, although it is not certain that the list is inclusive.[22]

In spite of his criticism, Downing ultimately found two areas in which Wheeler's book excelled. He conceded that it showed cultural and aesthetic discrimination, and he concurred with the other reviews as to the quality of Wheeler's presentation: "eminently readable, abounds with many excellent suggestions, especially as to matters of taste."

In addition to the reviews for *Rural Homes*, editors of what were termed eclectic journals exhibited sufficient interest in Wheeler's work to reprint illustrated excerpts. Among these, the *North American Miscellany* reprinted "The Suburban Villa" (see Figure 19), one of several essays from the pages of *The Home Journal*, which the "paper very decidedly and very justly commends . . . to its readers."[23] Similarly, *The Genessee Farmer* reproduced Wheeler's design and description for "A Suburban Cottage."[24] And *The Home Journal*, true to its cause, excerpted "The Present Metallic Age" from the pages of Wheeler's "admirable little book."[25]

Norwichtown, Connecticut, 1851–1852

Although Wheeler probably began to write the articles that eventually became *Rural Homes* in Philadelphia or Hartford, and the book was published in New York City, he signed the preface at Norwichtown, Connecticut. After only six months in New York, Wheeler turned up in the vicinity of Norwich, which may have been his wife's hometown. Whether this was in any way connected with his March correspondence with Richard Upjohn is unknown, but Upjohn had designed Christ Episcopal Church in Norwich, a work begun in 1846 that remained unfinished. While the church proper had been erected, the original drawings had called for a chapel wing and a freestanding tower. The chapel was finished by 1851 but lackluster fundraising for the tower ceased in July of that year and the project was abandoned. In that same month Upjohn wrote to Leonard Woods at Bowdoin to tell him that Wheeler was in Norwich

> interfering with my church there which is *unfinished for want of means* to carry out the design. In order that his mischievous pranks may be headed off I wish you to send some person in Norwich . . . some of the few particulars, pranks, and favours, with which you have been conversant . . . or send me something by which I may stop his capering.—do it forthwith.[1]

If previous experience is any indication, it would seem that Wheeler did not refrain from criticizing Upjohn's evolving project. Or perhaps he tried to sell the congregation a cheaper scheme. The relationship between the two architects, already a bit shaky, now seems to have fallen prey to a complete rift.

Woods promptly replied that while he himself would not volunteer information on Wheeler's past record, he could suggest a long list of names to whom the people of Norwich might address their inquiries as to Wheeler's reputation: Dr. Croswell of the Church of the Advent in Boston; George Sumner, M.D., of Trinity College in Hartford; George F. Dunning of the Mint of Philadelphia; his brother Reverend Andrew Dunning in Thompson, Connecticut, whom Woods had introduced to Wheeler over the course of their acquaintance in Brunswick; William Hoppin of New York; and Professor Smyth and Mr. McKeen of Brunswick. These men, if asked, would "put them on their guard about Mr. Wheeler."[2] That is a long list of widely scattered disgruntled clients or potential clients and acquaintances.

The exchange between Upjohn and Woods leaves much unexplained, but it was clearly an unequivocal disapproval of Wheeler's character, and an extension of the difficult relations at Bowdoin. There is no information about whether Upjohn used any of the references mentioned by Woods to sully Wheeler's local reputation, but Wheeler not only remained in the Norwich area for a while, he established an office there and produced some local work. From May to November 1852 he ran an ad in the *Norwich Weekly Courier* in which he gave the location of his office as Hubbard's Building, Main Street, Norwich. Addressing himself to those "contemplating building, arranging grounds or decorating the interior of their residences," and campaigning as always for the professional, he urged upon them "the advantage of obtaining the service of a disinterested and competent Architect," to produce plans, obtain a "more perfect mode of execution," and avoid litigation and dissatisfaction. He ended by listing "Churches, Public Buildings, Monuments, and all matters within the scope of his profession" as "faithfully attended to" at moderate price. There is no mention of his specialty, domestic design. In June 1852, an advertisement in the *Genessee Farmer* solicited "professional engagements from those desirous of building," this time mentioning residences as well as "churches, schoolhouses, arrangement of grounds and out-buildings and for internal decoration."[3] If he did ever produce such a wide-ranging variety of building types, no evidence of them has yet come to light.

JOSHUA NEWTON PERKINS HOUSE, NORWICH, CONNECTICUT

By his own testimony, Wheeler designed and saw erected at least one residence in the area. He must have been especially proud of it. He mentioned it in *Rural Homes*, suggesting a date of 1851,[4] and published it again as an "Italian Villa" or alternately a "Suburban Villa" in *The Horticulturalist* in 1853, and in *Homes for the People* in 1855, giving its location as outside of Norwich, and finally in *The Choice of a Dwelling*, published after his return to London (Figures 23, 24).[5]

It in fact remains standing, both house and grounds unfortunately altered, at 154 Washington Street, the road from Norwich to Norwichtown.[6] The house, an example of the then-fashionable Italianate mode in which the Picturesque profile joined forces with classical details, was designed probably as a summer home for Joshua Newton Perkins, a New York broker, on property he had owned at least since 1850 (Figure 25).[7] Constructed of painted brick dressed with Portland stone, with exterior details altered from the published view, it featured a tower and wooden verandas from which could be seen a "commanding prospect"; in fact, it still overlooks from its bluff the Yantic River and Holly Hock Island. In describing his design, Wheeler used the adjectives "picturesque" and "bold," and thought that the mass harmonized with the surrounding scenery—all notions

Figure 23.
*"Suburban Villa," Norwich, Connecticut.
(From* Homes for the People.*)*

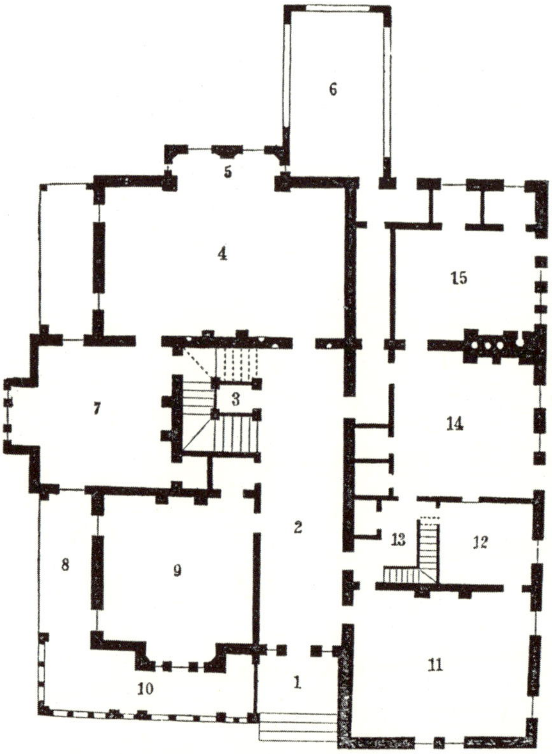

Figure 24.
*Plan of the "Suburban Villa," Norwich.
(From* Homes for the People.*)*

Figure 25.
Joshua Newton Perkins house, Norwich, ca. 1850–51.
(Tribert photo, 2009.)

Figure 26.
"Country Mansion in the Venetian Italian Style,"
said to have been erected below the hills of Berkshire County,
Massachusetts, ca. 1851–54. (From Homes for the People.*)*

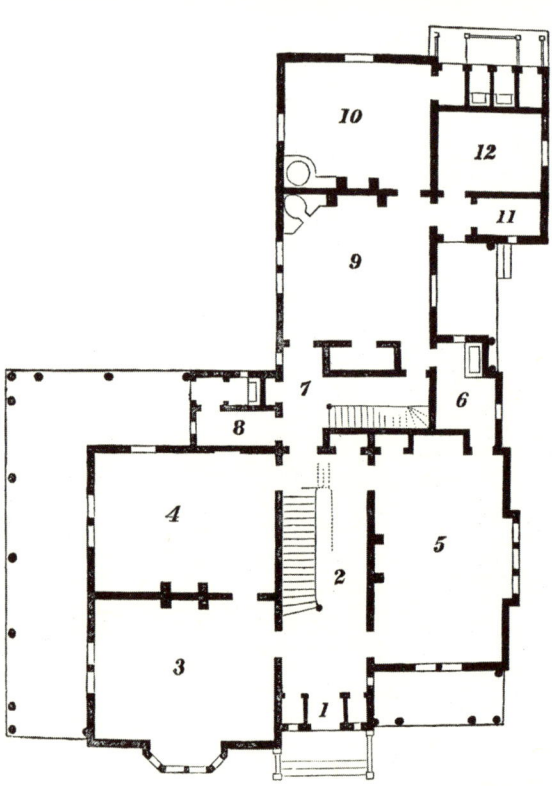

Figure 27.
*"Cottage Ornée," erected on the Housatonic River in the Berkshires, ca. 1851–54.
(From* Homes for the People.*)*

Figure 28.
*Plan of the "Cottage Ornée."
(From* Homes for the People.*)*

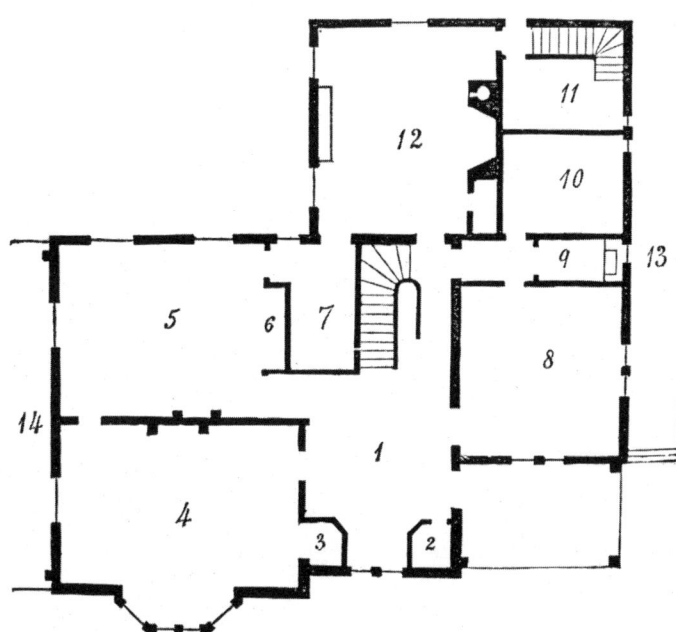

Figure 29.
"Cottage Villa," Lenox Road, near Stockbridge, Massachusetts, 1851–54. (From Homes for the People.*)*

Figure 30.
Plan of a "Cottage Villa." (From Homes for the People.*)*

in keeping with the Picturesque esthetic and with Wheeler's own conception of appropriate rural domestic architecture.

Many of the commissions previously discussed have been documented by primary source material other than Wheeler's writings. In addition to these, there are a number of residential designs that Wheeler claimed to have undertaken, particularly in his *Homes for the People* of 1855. He cited a number of residences as executed, presumably during the years between his first and second books. The commissions were located in areas such as the Housatonic Hills of Berkshire County, Massachusetts; the outskirts of Norwich, Connecticut; Orange, New Jersey; along the Long Island Sound in New York; and overlooking the Hudson River.

Due to their locations, and knowing of his advertisement in *The Genessee Farmer* at this time (which might have reached an audience in the Berkshires, for instance), it is possible that a number of these designs were undertaken while Wheeler was practicing in Norwichtown. They include a country mansion in the "Venetian Italian style," "in a noble farm below the hills of Berkshire County (Figure 26);[8] a "Cottage Ornée" on the summit of a peak along the Housatonic in the Berkshires (Figures 27, 28);[9] and a "Cottage Villa," one mile from Stockbridge on the Lenox Road, also in Berkshire County (Figures 29, 30).

While Wheeler suggests generalized locations for these houses, which to date have not been identified, he also illustrates and discusses other designs for which he gives no address, either because they were never built or the owners wished for privacy. Whether or not any of these houses still stand remains to be seen.

New York City, 1853–1860

Wheeler continued to roam during these years, as he had since his arrival in America. Most notable among his trips was a return to Europe, perhaps near the end of 1852. Little is known of this, though Wheeler specifically mentioned visiting London.[1] Whatever the reason for the journey, by July 1853 he was back in the United States. A notice in *The Horticulturist* announced: "The friends of Gervase Wheeler, the accomplished architect and author of *Rural Homes*, will be glad to learn that he has returned from Europe and resumed the practice of his profession."[2] The notice was supplemented by ads placed by Wheeler in the August and November issues of the same magazine.[3]

Wheeler returned to New York City, where directories consistently listed his residence as 1 Elm Place, Brooklyn, a middle-class neighborhood, while he frequently changed offices. According to the *American Architect* for 1884, Henry Hudson Holly (1834–1892) apprenticed with him from 1854 until leaving for England in 1856. On his return Holly briefly joined in practice Charles Duggin (1830–1916), another immigrant. The subsequent work of both would show Wheeler's influence.[4]

Holly worked with Wheeler at the time the latter was writing his second book, *Homes for the People, in Suburb and Country; The Villa, the Mansion, and the Cottage, Adapted to American Climate and Wants* (1855). It is safe to suggest that, if Holly did not in fact collaborate on the volume, he was familiar with the ideas and designs that Wheeler espoused. In the preface of his *Country Seats*, Holly noted that "the work was fully prepared for the press some two years since," but its publication was hindered by the outbreak of the Civil War. In other words, Holly had drafted his book in late 1860 and early 1861, soon after Wheeler's departure for England.

The content and organization of *Homes for the People* will be discussed later, but some of the similarities between these two architects' published works bear mention here. Both addressed the general public as opposed to an audience of architects and builders. *Country Seats* began, as had *Homes for the People*, with a brief history of architecture, and devoted several pages to a differentiation of the types of homes sought by differing classes of people. Several of Holly's designs, though modified in plan, presented combinations of motifs or proportions reminiscent of Wheeler's work in *Homes for the People*. As the book's audience represented prospective clients, Holly, like Wheeler, championed hiring an architect for the planning of a country house. He also followed Wheeler's example in noting that the designs were "not intended for model houses, to be copied for all localities, but simply to show how important it is to have an original design adapted to the peculiarities of site."[5]

Beyond the similarities in their books, Holly also shaped a professional course similar to Wheeler's. Both designed executed buildings, but relied upon publication to popularize their domestic projects. Repeating a pattern set by Wheeler a quarter of a century earlier, in 1876 Holly began contributing a series of articles entitled "Modern Dwellings, Their Construction, Decoration and Furniture" to *Harper's New Monthly Magazine*.[6] The series would become the foundation for his second book, *Modern Dwellings*, published in 1878.[7] The most conspicuous difference between the careers of the two men lay in organizational associations. Unlike Wheeler, Holly was from the outset involved in the A.I.A. and was elected to Fellowship in 1858, even before Wheeler's departure.

As we have seen, in 1855 Charles Scribner issued Wheeler's second book. The author had in fact been working on the volume since 1852, but he tells us that the manuscript and all related papers, including the illustrations, were destroyed in a fire in 1854.[8] One of the designs he published in *A Book of Plans* of 1853 had been intended for this publication. The work was taken up again, from memory, according to the author. Wheeler noted that the impetus for publishing anew lay in the numerous requests for assistance and professional advice "from all parts of the country," which, if true, suggests his popular appeal and the considerable success of his first book. But Wheeler's desire to publish may also have meant a lack of sufficient commissions in his architectural practice.

When Wheeler wrote his first book, he was at the forefront of Picturesque architectural expression in this country. The book had mirrored the romanticism of the mode in its stylistic presentation. He now adopted a more practical format. More than one hundred pages longer than *Rural Homes*, this second book also contained many more illustrations. It reflected Wheeler's broader experience in the American market and included twice as many executed residences as the first book. The simpler, more compact silhouettes of his earlier designs gave way to richer Picturesque compositions. A comparison of his Suburban Villa from *Rural Homes* (see Figure 19) with the Suburban Villa in *Homes for the People* (see Figure 23) makes the point.

In *Homes for the People*, Wheeler defined various manifestations of the villa, the mansion, and the cottage as different domestic types, and elaborated on other residential programs, both expensive and modest. Modes of construction also engaged his interest, including the particularly American balloon frame, "a novel mode of constructing cheap wooden dwellings." He also devoted a separate chapter to the historical background and development of various architectural manifestations such as the Gothic and the Italian. In discussing the projects themselves, he stressed the importance of achieving "unity of effect" within the design and between house and landscape, a theme carried through from his first writings. Drawing on his interest in interior decoration to a greater extent than in *Rural Homes*, Wheeler sketched in detail his ideas for the interior decor for many of the projects, although he shows neither interior perspectives nor elevations. Several of the illustrated designs had appeared previously, such as that for a Suburban Villa, erected near Norwich, illustrated in the August 1853 issue of *The Horticulturist* (see Figure 23)[9] or "A Villa Mansion in the Italian Style" which appeared months later in the pages of the same journal (Figures 31, 32).[10]

The reviews for this second book proved again fairly consistent, with approbation for the style and presentation of the material and its practical contents. *The Horticulturist* remarked upon the attractive illustrations and practical arrangement of chapters and continued with a compliment on Wheeler's writing skills, and his "faculty of expressing his ideas in refined and very agreeable language."[11] Another review in a popular journal considered the work a compendium of useful suggestions on construction and "carefully-digested plans."[12] *The Knickerbocker* praised Wheeler's juxtaposition of designs with text, thereby keeping the interest of the general reader.[13] Showing their continued support, *The Home Journal* editors included a portion of the work in their columns and commended "the ease and graceful style of Mr. Wheeler's writing" (12 March 1855). The editors also made reference to the popularity of *Homes for the People* by noting that Scribner had published the book at a low price, thus prompting high sales (2 June). The *Boston Evening Transcript* ended its short notice by affirming that if "the suggestions of Mr. Wheeler and those found in Downing's books are heeded there will be a great change in the appearance and comfort of dwellings in our country."[14] In the mind of that reviewer at least, Wheeler had reached a stature equal to that of Downing.

The only hostile review, but a serious one, came from the editors of *The Builder* of London. It scathingly accused Wheeler of plagiarism. International copyright laws did not exist at this time, and though many authors like Dickens lobbied for them, the practice of adopting source material into one's own texts was widespread. *The Builder* apparently considered Wheeler's plagiarism unusually bold: "the author has appropriated the writings of others in the most extraordinary manner, without the slightest acknowledgment."[15] The anonymous critic substantiated his accusation by running passages from *Homes for the People* side by side with the anonymous work entitled "History in Ruins—A Handbook of Architecture for the Unlearned," previously published as a series in the magazine. Indeed, in each case, Wheeler's words reproduce in remarkably similar terms, though with embellished vocabulary, the thoughts of the original work. Although

Figure 31.
"Villa Mansion in the Italian Style," erected between Rye and Portchester on Long Island Sound, ca. 1851–54. (From Homes for the People.*)*

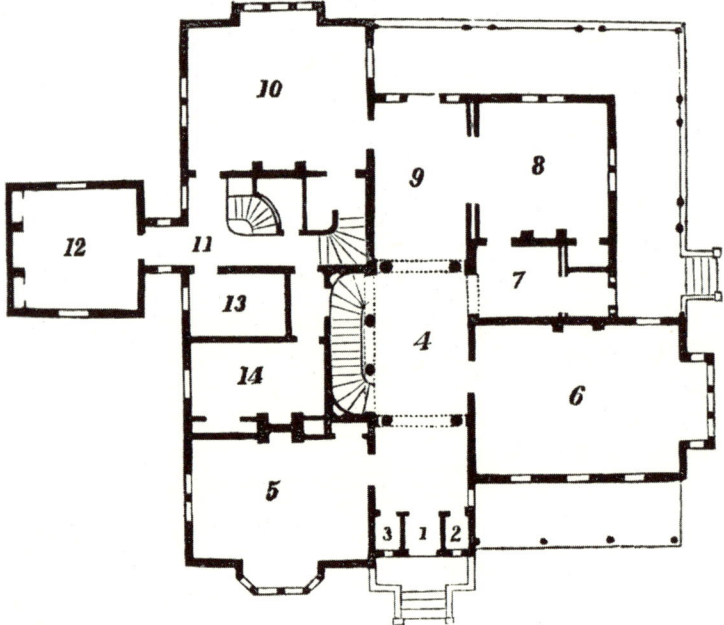

Figure 32.
Plan of a "Villa Mansion." (From Homes for the People.*)*

none of this affected his message about Picturesque domestic design, again we have a glimpse of the darker side of his character.

In addition to his own books, Wheeler occasionally submitted designs and articles for publication in other journals and books. Wheeler's "Villa in the Tudor Style" (see Figure 9) reappeared in the 1849 volume of *The Horticulturist*, as we have noted; this was followed in 1853 by a design for an Italian villa, and in 1855 with "A Villa Mansion." Downing had criticized Wheeler's *Rural Homes*, as we know, and may have been disappointed by the latter's professional conduct. His sponsorship ended in 1851, and Wheeler's other contributions to *The Horticulturalist* appeared only after Downing's death in 1852. In May 1855, *The Horticulturist* reproduced a "Villa Mansion" from the pages of *Homes for the People* (see Figures 31, 32).[16] Wheeler wrote that the house had been erected on a site overlooking the Long Island Sound, between Rye and Portchester, New York. In the Italian style, it was designed with the very specific needs of the client in mind: a sloping prospect that required terracing and a plan that facilitated family entertaining.

UNNAMED TOWNHOUSE, NEW YORK CITY

During his six years and more in the city, Wheeler presumably designed buildings for New York, but we have at this writing a glimpse of only one of them. It was a grand urban residence that adopted, he said, the Parisian rather than the London model. In *The Choice of Dwelling* he gives the principal and bedroom plans of a "spacious New York house by the author" erected on a large lot at the corner of two wide streets (Figure 33). On the main floor, the drawing room occupies the entire front while the anteroom, the library, and the dining room embrace the central vestibule and stair. There is a basement with billiard room beneath the drawing room, and three floors of bedchambers beneath a mansard for the servants.[17] We have no other information about this intriguing design.

PROJECT FOR A CONGREGATIONAL CHURCH

In 1853 the Congregational Churches of America produced *A Book of Plans for Churches and Parsonages* to provide drawings, specifications, and estimates promoting "convenience, economy, and good taste" to congregations contemplating the building of frontier churches.[18] At a convention held in Albany in October 1852 a committee of ministers solicited projects from ten architects, including Henry Austin, Henry Cleaveland, James Renwick, Jr., Richard Upjohn, and

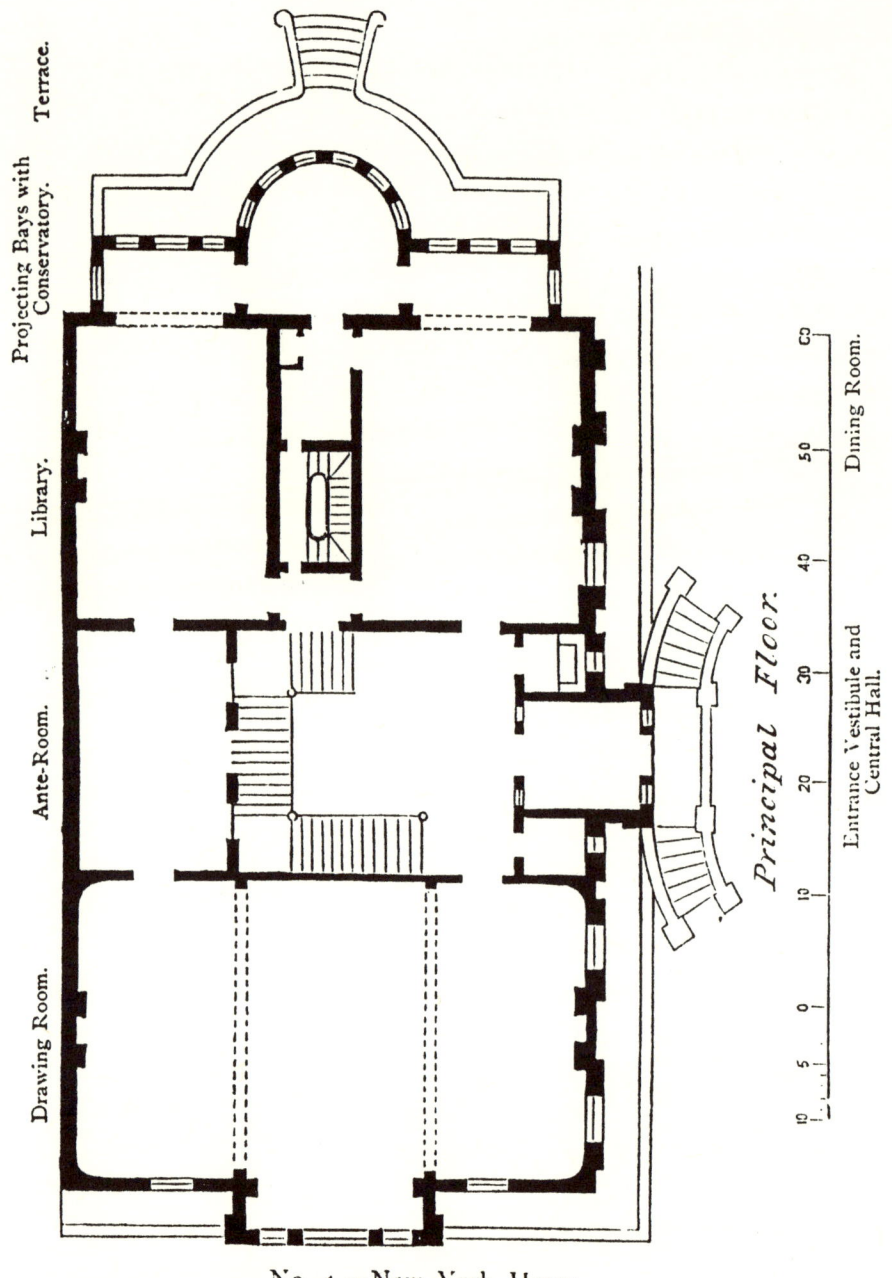

Figure 33.
*Plan of an unnamed townhouse,
New York City, 1850s.
(From* The Choice
of a Dwelling.*)*

Gervase Wheeler, all but two of them New Yorkers. Wheeler here found himself among the leaders of the profession.

The entries by Wheeler included a church and two parsonages. Although the convention generally espoused the round-arched style for the Congregationalists, Wheeler was not alone in proposing a Gothic model for his church (Design XV). It was to be a cruciform frame building that could hold about 550 people. It provided for the needs of a village or frontier town by allowing for timber construction, which Wheeler considered the most readily available material. The various community activities were gathered under a single roof: worship space, schoolroom, and library opposite a study and vestry for the minister, and a lecture room on the upper floor.

This is the only known published ecclesiastical design of Wheeler's career in America.[19] The front elevation was to be asymmetrical, with tower-belfry-spire rising on the left adjacent to the paired and hooded entrance doors centered on the roof ridge. A shift in the slope of the roof over the sides of the main block reflected the aisles within. Although Gothic Revival in style, with pointed openings and ornamental tracery and drip moldings enriching the "upright plank and battened joints" of the exterior, an Ecclesiologist project it was not. And it contradicted something Wheeler himself had just published in what seems perhaps a vengeful swipe at Upjohn: "One of our best architects, and one who, of all others, has had the largest and most liberal freedom for the expression of his designs, almost always makes his churches on one stereotyped plan, cruciform and with a broken-backed roof. A church in the form of a cross is beautiful . . . if *vast*; but on a small scale, such a plan is unwarrantable and . . . is done so very ignorantly."[20]

One of the parsonage houses published in this book was an adaptation of a design prepared for *Homes for the People*. No. III, in an Italian mode, corresponded to "A Small Villa," while No. IV represented "A Rustic Parsonage."[21] In concluding his contribution to the book, Wheeler offered his services to those considering erecting his designs: "if any further explanation can help its erection in the numerous church-settlements of the growing west, a letter to the publishers of this work, addressed to G. Wheeler, Architect, will cheerfully be replied to."

THE FIRST PRESBYTERIAN CHURCH, OWEGO, NEW YORK

The Presbyterian congregation in Owego laid the "foundation stone" of its new church in June 1854 and began to worship in the building a year later.[22] A stone tablet set high into the south face of the south tower reads

Figure 34.
*First Presbyterian Church, Owego. Interior in 1884.
(Courtesy Gary Murray.)*

FIRST PRESBYTERIAN CHURCH.
ERECTED A. D. 1854.
GERVASE WHEELER.
ARCHITECT
C. HUNGERFORD. BUILDER.[23]

The local paper also credited the work to "Architect, Gervase Wheeler, Esq., of New York," whose project bested "quite a number of designs . . . prepared by different architects." It also described the building as "elegant and singular in its design, different from any structure in any of our neighboring villages. At first the architectural dimensions and wood work appear too light for a solid permanent building, but when a person investigates the principles upon which it is constructed, its permanency and strength will appear sufficient" (Figure 34). Hot air furnaces eliminated the need for a "stove or stove-pipes to mar the beauty or obstruct the view" of the 800-seat interior. This openness was enhanced by the lack of galleries. The design of "stained and figured window glass" is also attributed to Wheeler in the paper, but it would appear that the colored glass now *in situ* is later.[24]

This ecclesiastical work shows marked improvement over Wheeler's earlier Gothic church at Berlin, Connecticut; differs dramatically from the carpenter Gothic design he submitted to *A Book of Plans*; and varies from his next ecclesiastical design, Gothic Goodrich Hall, the Williams College Chapel. If for the Congregationalists' book he stuck to Gothic, for the Presbyterians of Owego he used the round-arched style, with solid brick exterior walls enclosing a three-aisled section with clerestory, the aisles separated from the nave by delicate arches on thin octagonal columns. The gable roof is supported by airy timbered trusses. Although the church has been altered,[25] its original plan is apparent. This was a broad rectangle with a narthex between the towers fronted by a projecting triple-arched porch, no transepts, and no recess beyond the reading desk; it was, in short, more like an eighteenth-century New England meeting house than a Gothic church. Once again his criticism of Upjohn's ecclesiastical work seems shallow.

The present low exterior silhouette is not original, for early twentieth-century postcard views, while they are a bit fuzzy, do show a tall spire rising from the third story of the northern tower (the configuration of the present third story is also not original), while the southern tower ended above its present stump in a domed kiosk-like form much lower than the spire (Figure 35). The irregular profile, found in many a Gothic Revival church, contrasted with the balanced classical detail of the round-arched entrance porch with axial pediment supported by brackets and the segmental blind arcades of the lower side walls framing half-round arched windows. Such a use of low-relief blind brick arcading recalls the work of Charles Bulfinch rather than that of R. C. Carpenter, and may reflect the contemporary New England revival of Federal forms in ecclesiastical architecture (Figure 36).[26] In any event, in this work Wheeler seems far from his English Gothic roots.

CHAPEL, WILLIAMS COLLEGE, WILLIAMSTOWN, MASSACHUSETTS

Ten years after his experience at Bowdoin College, Wheeler again had the opportunity to work on a multipurpose educational building, this one containing a chapel, alumni hall, and classrooms. The building has been called Goodrich Hall since the early twentieth century and now houses the student center. Much as had been the case at Bowdoin, by the mid-nineteenth century the Trustees of Williams College were in need of enlarged facilities. In 1856, they resolved to build them.

Figure 35.
*First Presbyterian Church,
Owego. Present condition.
(O'Gorman photo, 2009.)*

Figure 36.
*First Presbyterian Church,
Owego. Detail of exterior.
(O'Gorman photo, 2009.)*

There is no information about the selection of the architect or the choice of the style. It is unlikely that Wheeler was recommended by Bowdoin's Leonard Woods, given the latter's letter written to Richard Upjohn about Wheeler's interference at Norwich. At any rate, in July 1857 Wheeler wrote beneath his New York letterhead to the Reverend Calvin Durfee at Williams indicating that he had already produced a design for the building. According to campus rumor it was to be "a structure of Gothic proportions" that would "ornament our College."[27] After reviewing the plan, the Trustees requested that the length of the chapel be increased by five feet. In order to accommodate this change, Wheeler advised them that the design submitted could simply be adapted: in plan, by extending the building the extra five feet, and in elevation, by raising the height of the gable. In this way, the chapel would retain the appropriate roof pitch and proper architectural proportions.

One week later, Reverend Durfee and Professor Mark Hopkins, president of the College, indicated that the Trustees had now decided upon a rear addition, Alumni Hall, measuring 33 feet by 28 feet, and changing the plan to a cross. Wheeler then wrote that whether one story or two, such an addition to the existing

Figure 37.
*Williams College Chapel,
Williamstown, Massachusetts, 1856–59.
Preliminary perspective view.
(Courtesy of Williams College
Archives and Special Collections.)*

scheme would so alter it as to require new drawings: "In view of these additions and alterations [including perhaps enlarging the tower when 'I see the building as intended upon paper'], I must in justice to myself insist that before any thing in the way of *actual* commencement be made of the building, I be instructed to prepare new plans—these alterations so materially affecting the whole spirit of the design." He continued, "With this under my control I see no difficulty in reconciling such additions with architectural propriety & beauty."[28]

Wheeler requested that the first set of plans be returned to him before he advanced a reworked design. The Trustees apparently complied, and in October his revised drawings and specifications were available at the college for the inspection of prospective builders. In what may have been another swipe at Upjohn, he told the locals that "the structure, when completed, will be the finest connected with any College in the country." Wheeler's involvement apparently ended with the paper project; as was typical for his career, he did not supervise the execution of the building.

The location of the original and revised drawings, as well as the specifications, is unknown, but there exists in College Archives a copy of a perspective view of the chapel that must be preliminary. The alumni addition is present but the elevated site is depicted as flat and the top of the tower is not as finally erected (Figure 37).

Construction began in April 1858, and contrary to the described 33-by-28-foot extension to the rear of the chapel, the addition built was in fact 36 feet by 56 feet, and resulted in a T-shaped plan instead of the cruciform noted by Wheeler. It remains unknown to what extent he had a hand in these final changes. The Chapel, dedicated in September 1859, in a rural Gothic but hardly Ecclesiological mode since Williams College had Congregational leanings, was built of local bluish-gray limestone laid in rough ashlar (Figures 38, 39). The gable roof was covered in slate, and a stone tower rose off to the side, projecting heavenward 95 feet to the tip of its wooden spire, and providing stairway access to the alumni hall above ground-floor classrooms. Window openings and doorways were expressed as pointed arches, although in the tower Wheeler placed a pointed opening above a segmental one above a narrow trabeated window above a slightly pointed doorway, thus "showing off his knowledge of all kinds of arches."[29] The original interior with its lack of ornamental embellishment was more austere than Wheeler's round-arched design at Owego, although he repeated the airy trusses he used in the earlier church and preserved the openness found there.

The Williams building has undergone alterations over the years, from enlargement of the windows to renovation of the stairs and tower. The interior has been thoroughly worked over, although the trusses now in place seem original. In the early twentieth century and again in the 1920s, changes in use, and substantive changes to the structure, including the removal of the spire and the northwest vestibule and porch, have significantly altered the expression of Wheeler's original project (Figure 40).

DESIGNS FOR A "COUNTRY BANK"

This period also saw Wheeler in rare contemplation of a commercial building type and once more resorting to the printing press to spread his name abroad. In April 1856 *The Bankers' Magazine and Statistical Register*, published in New York by I. Smith Homans, printed his "Architecture of Country Banks."[30] This was the leading financial periodical of its day.[31] Catering to a broad banking community, it provided contiguous services, such as designs for banking facilities. Wheeler must have viewed it as a good place to advertise his wares.

The article, largely devoted to the kind of nuts-and-bolts approach to buildings favored by Wheeler, also featured two alternate designs, and addressed what

Figure 38.
*Williams College Chapel,
as originally built.
(Courtesy of Williams College
Archives and Special Collections.)*

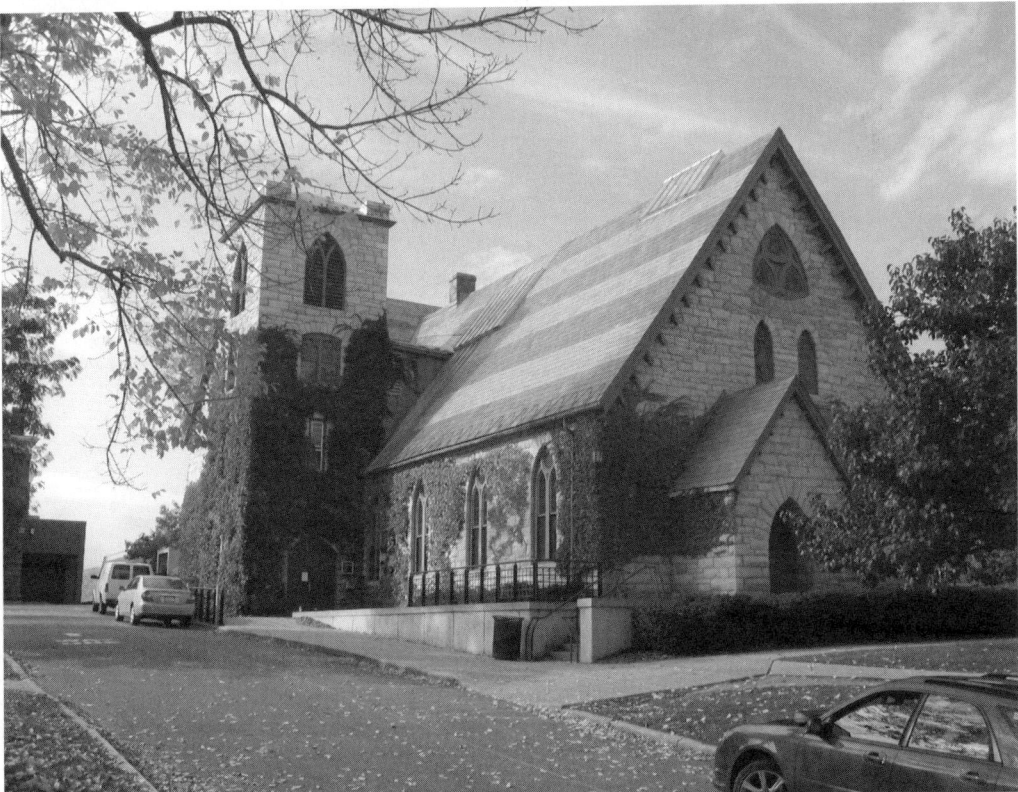

Figure 39. (top) *Interior of Williams College Chapel in the 1850s. (Courtesy of Williams College Archives and Special Collections.)*
Figure 40. (bottom) *Williams College Chapel (now Goodrich Hall) as altered. (O'Gorman photo, 2006)*

[79

Figure 41.
*Design for a country bank.
(From* The Bankers' Magazine, *April 1856.)*

Figure 42.
*Alternate design for a country bank.
(From* The Bankers' Magazine, *April 1856.)*

the architect saw as the sorely neglected need of rural banking for an architecture reflecting its environment. Invoking the canonical theme of fitness, Wheeler proposed that country banks acquire their own architectural expression, instead of applying traditionally used urban motifs. His designs were intended to achieve "individual character," adaptation to "circumstances of locality," "convenient and sensible building," and "harmony with its expressed intention." In terms of style, these conditions could best be realized in either classic or modern Italian. Gothic, "the dead styles" of early Greece and Egypt, and the "Lombardic" he judged unsuitable for the type. Despite such a premise, it is difficult to find environmental fitness in the designs shown in the plates Wheeler published with the text (Figures 41, 42). These exhibit variant Italianate façades that, were their designer unknown, could as easily be assigned to Philadelphia's John Notman, Boston's Hammatt Billings, New Haven's Henry Austin, New York's Minard Lafever, or any number of other urban architects practicing in the 1850s.[32] Whether either of these designs were ever realized remains a question.

DRAWINGS FOR AN ITALIANATE VILLA

Churches and banks might occasionally have come from Wheeler's drafting board, but residential design remained his mainstay. A small number of domestic works from this period, other than those Wheeler himself published, have come to light; certainly there were many others. The Library of Congress, for example, has a bound album of seven drawings for an Italianate villa that Wheeler executed while his office was in the Nassau Bank Building on Beekman Street; that is, in 1855. The cover is labeled GERVASE WHEELER/ARCHITECT/NEW YORK and his name and address appear on all the drawings. No client is mentioned, but the orientations given to the elevations suggest a specific site.[33]

The design is a reduced version of Henry Austin's contemporary Morse mansion in Portland, Maine, and there were many other similar villas erected in various parts of the country or published in this period. The main floor plan is centered on the hall leading from the entrance to the stair and kitchen, with parlor to one side, dining room and library to the other. Above the entrance rises a three-story tower flanked by a low-gabled two-story salient with half-octagon bay off the parlor to the right, and library-dining room wing off to the left behind a porch. The eaves are bracketed; the pair of round-arched windows at the second level of the tower anticipate those Wheeler was to use in his nearly contemporary Barry house in Rochester.

THE PATRICK BARRY HOUSE, ROCHESTER, NEW YORK

Wheeler's contributions to *The Horticulturist* and *The Genessee Farmer* suggest the way he obtained this Rochester commission. Patrick Barry, an Irish immigrant teacher, turned his attention to horticulture in 1840 and established a nursery in Rochester with George Ellwanger. His enthusiasm and abilities, undoubtedly enhanced by his experience as an educator, led by 1844 to the editorship of *The Genessee Farmer*, a position he held until 1852. After A. J. Downing's death, Barry filled the same post at *The Horticulturist* from 1852 to 1854.[34] He published Wheeler's contributions during his tenure as editor of both magazines.

When Barry's earlier dwelling burned in October 1856, he turned to Wheeler for the design of his new house. It is not clear whether the two men actually met, or if Barry's familiarity with Wheeler's published work led him to the commission. The Ellwanger and Barry Nursery records show that construction began early in 1857 and final payments were made in January 1859. For his design, Wheeler was paid a lump sum of $95 "for paym. of a/c."[35] In other words, Wheeler's commission seems to have been limited to design drawings.[36] This inference is further supported by a documented payment in 1858 of $300 to Austin and Warner, Rochester architects (this Austin, Merwin, was the brother of Henry with whom Wheeler had worked in New Haven; Andrew Jackson Warner was his [and thus Henry's] nephew). They supervised the construction and may well have influenced the final appearance of the house.[37]

Barry's house is an Italian villa in rose-red brick, a material that Wheeler noted could be used in country buildings "with good advantage."[38] The house was surveyed by the Historic American Buildings Survey in 1969. The irregularly massed profile includes verandas and a campanile of two stories, square in plan, surmounted by an octagonal third floor topped by a peaked, swooping roof (Figures 43, 44). The eaves are bracketed, and the windows framed by distinctive arched limestone moldings. Much as in Wheeler's previous plans, the communicating library and parlor, which open onto verandas, stand across the entry hall from the service wing. Interior appointments include marble fireplaces, grained woodwork, and ornamental plaster ceilings. The Provost's office at the University of Rochester now occupies the house.

Figure 43.
Patrick Barry House,
Rochester, New York, 1856–58.
(Hans Padelt for the Historic American
Buildings Survey, 1968.)

Figure 44.
Barry House. Interior in 1968.
(Hans Padelt for the Historic American
Buildings Survey, 1968.)

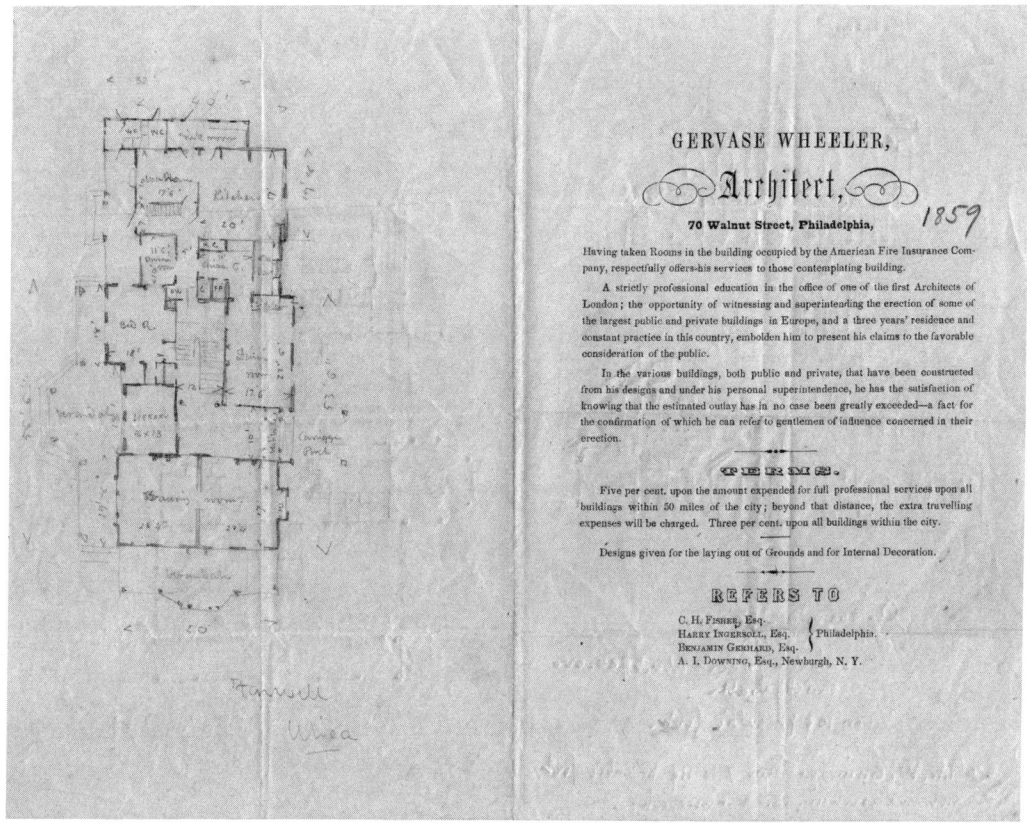

Figure 45.
*O. Farwell house (project?), Utica, New York,
ca. 1855–58. First floor plan on reverse of fig. 46.
(Warshaw Collection of Business of Business Americana-Architecture,
Archives Center, National Museum of American History,
Smithsonian Institution.)*

PROJECT FOR THE O. FARWELL HOUSE, UTICA, NEW YORK

The rough sketches for a house intended for O. Farwell at Utica, as yet otherwise unidentified, likely date from this period as well. These, two plans and two elevations, occur on both sides of a copy of the advertising flyer Wheeler had printed in Philadelphia at the beginning of the decade, but they clearly do not coincide with that date (Figures 45, 46).[39] They envision a large and elaborate brick Italianate villa estimated to cost $20,000 rising from a characteristic Wheeler elongated plan, in this case akin but not identical to that for a "Southern Mansion" published in *Homes for the People*.[40] The rooms gather on two floors around a central stair hall surmounted by a skylight. Arched verandahs spread the mass

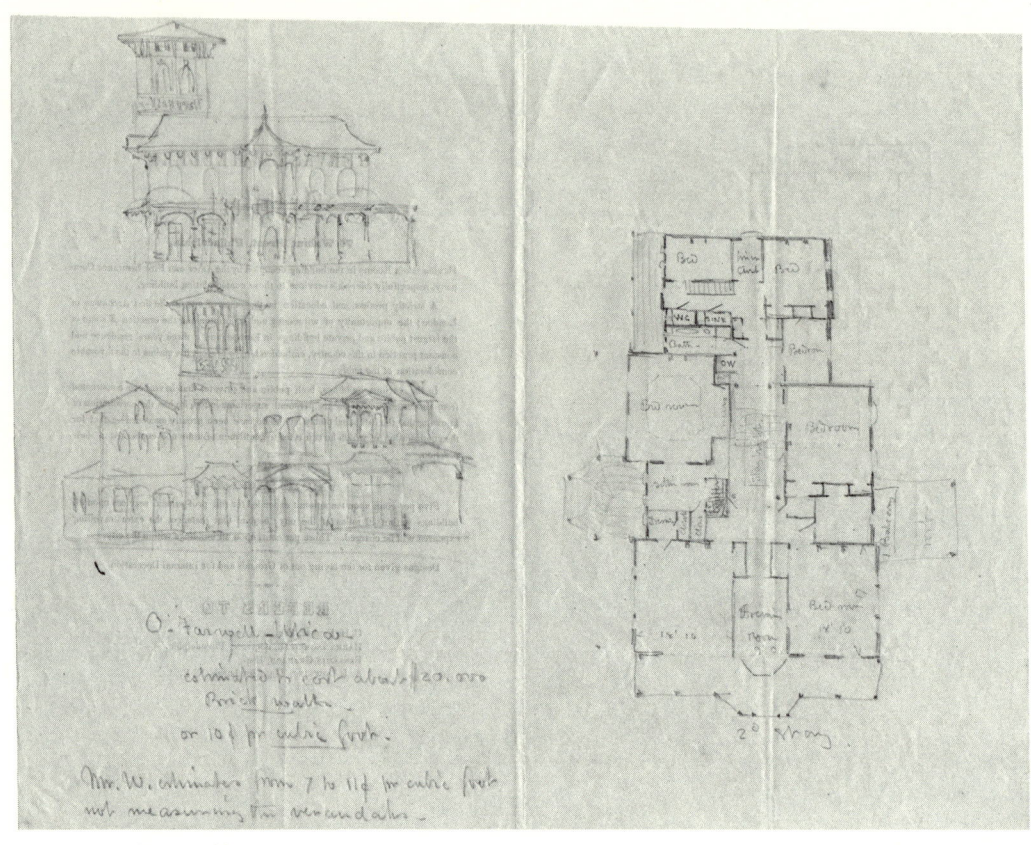

Figure 46.
O. Farwell house. Elevations and second floor plan on Wheeler advertisement, ca. 1855–58. (Warshaw Collection of Business of Business Americana-Architecture, Archives Center, National Museum of American History, Smithsonian Institution.)

on the ground; a three-story tower topped by a belvedere with double openings on each side enriches the skyline.

PROJECT FOR PROFESSOR JOHN TATLOCK'S GROUNDS, WILLIAMSTOWN

One train of events at Bowdoin College seemed to repeat itself at Williams College. Wheeler had apparently managed to establish relations with members of the college community while working on the drawings for the Chapel. In his letter of 14 July 1857 to Rev. Durfee, he referred to a project for Professor John Tatlock, at that date teaching mathematics at the college. Wheeler asked Durfee to check with Tatlock to see if he had received a "plan . . . for his grounds" sent express two weeks earlier. He is concerned that it may not have reached its destination.[41] Whether it did, and whether anything came of that project, remains lost to history, but what seems to be one example of Wheeler's work of this sort has come to light. This is an unsigned, undated, and unidentified sketch of the garden plan for a house that probably dates from the last half of the 1850s.[42] It shows a characteristic Wheeler extended domestic plan in a landscape setting of evergreens, a kitchen garden, and an orchard on a corner lot. The predominance of the orchard might reflect Wheeler's use of Patrick Barry's *The Fruit Garden*, a work we know he recommended. Diagonal lines indicate a concern for how the place would be viewed from the corner. Surely other such evidence of this kind lurks in various archives.

PROJECT FOR BUSHNELL PARK, HARTFORD

Wheeler had advertised more than once that among his skills was the "arrangement of grounds": in 1849 in the Hartford City Directory,[43] in the advertising flyer he had printed while in Philadelphia in 1850 ("Designs given for the laying out of Grounds"),[44] and in 1852 in the *Norwich Weekly Courier* and *The Genessee Farmer*.[45] In an ad in the original edition of his *Homes for the People* of 1855 he said he was prepared to give designs in "Rural Architecture and Landscape Gardening." The correspondence regarding Professor Tatlock's grounds is, however, the only document now known that mentions such a project. It was followed a year later by another landscaping effort, this time a larger scheme for the city of Hartford.

In 1858, the city proposed the creation of a public park, to be named after Horace Bushnell, eloquent teacher and minister of the North Congregational Church from 1833 to 1859.[46] Bushnell led the movement to establish a city park as early as 1853. A design competition was organized in order to solicit ideas. Wheeler submitted a plan that was awarded first prize from among twelve participants. It may be that his familiarity with Hartford people from years before helped him to achieve a winning entry.

Despite its esthetic merits, the city committee considered Wheeler's scheme too expensive to implement, and recommended that it be combined with the design of the second-place entrant, Seth Marsh, the city engineer. This plan also integrated elements from a third proposal. As construction of the new park progressed, the commission considered that it lacked an overall unity and beauty, and in 1861 (after Wheeler's return to England) hired the pioneering professional landscape architect Jacob Weidenmann to make alterations. Wheeler's original plan for the park is no longer extant. A map in the Hartford Park Papers, thought to have been rendered in 1858, shows what may have been the revised version by Marsh. It is unfortunately now impossible to evaluate the merits of Wheeler's ideas.[47]

MISCELLANEOUS EXECUTED DESIGNS

According to the architect's own testimony, he had completed a number of other domestic designs by 1855 while he practiced in New York. These included, as we have seen, an elaborate townhouse in the city, mentioned in *The Choice of a Dwelling*,[48] and a "Southern Mansion" in a "midland state" (Figures 47, 48), with "domestic offices semi-detached from the building," an arrangement common in the South, but with nothing that would make it unsuitable to the North. Although the irregular or Picturesque silhouette seems overdone, he as usual gives a functional explanation for it. Thus the roof of the main tower

> is formed to resist heat, and is contrived also to form a means of ventilation . . . [via] air-ducts, communicating with each [lower room], discharging into the large receptacle . . . formed between . . . roof and the flat ceiling of the upper room . . . and being dispersed into the atmosphere by means of apertures . . . [in the roof] protected from the weather by a proper mode of construction.[49]

He also illustrates a "Rustic Villa" erected in Orange, New Jersey[50] (Figures 49, 50), a rather ordinary "Square Cottage," erected in two places near the Hudson River (Figures 51, 52), and the remodeling of a country home overlooking the Hudson River (Figure 53). The difficulty of locating any house from these vague descriptions has prohibited confirmation of their execution but suggests future possibilities for research at the local level.

Figure 47.
"Southern Mansion," ca. 1851–54.
(*From* Homes for the People.)

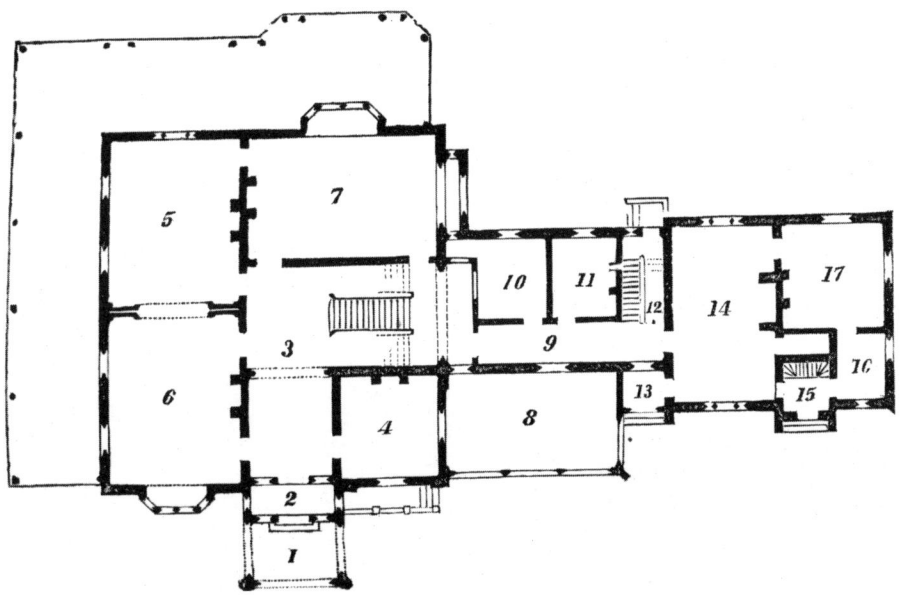

Figure 48.
Plan of "Southern Mansion."
(*From* Homes for the People.)

[89]

Figure 49.
"Rustic Villa," Orange, New Jersey, ca. 1851–54.
(*From* Homes for the People.)

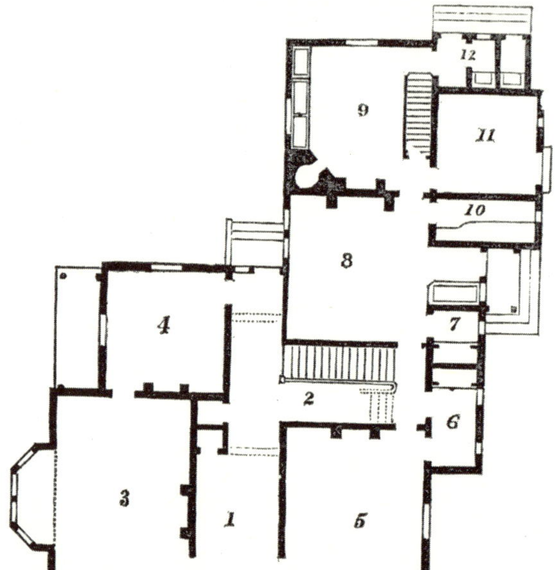

Figure 50.
Plan of the "Rustic Villa."
(*From* Homes for the People.)

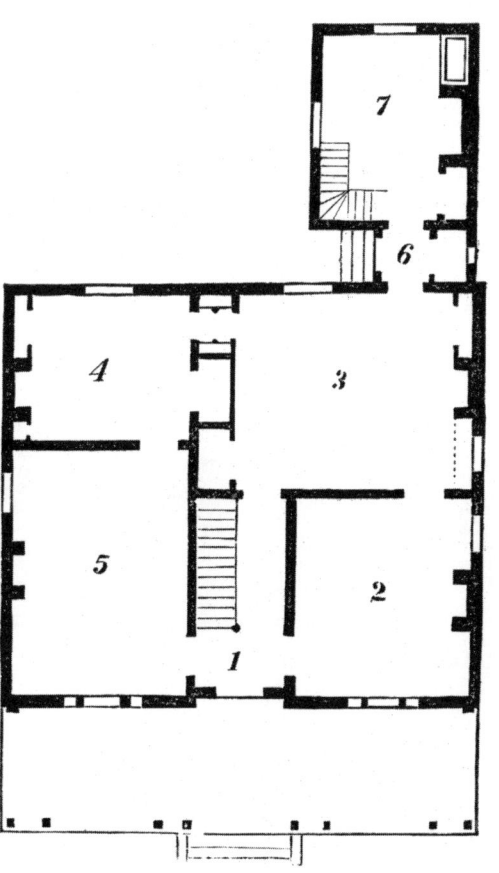

Figure 51.
"Square Cottage," near Hudson, New York, ca. 1851–54.
(*From* Homes for the People.)

Figure 52.
Plan of "Square Cottage."
(*From* Homes for the People.)

Figure 53.
*Remodeled "Country House"
overlooking the Hudson, ca. 1853–54.
(From* Homes for the People.*)*

Wheeler gives in his publications other projects from before 1855 for which there is no stated location. These range from "The Cheap Home" to the cottage to elaborate estates. An example of the former would be the Tudor Gothic parsonage discussed in *Homes for the People*. His statement that it was "attached to an Episcopal church in Massachusetts" is even vaguer than those locations given above (Figure 54).[51] The next group includes an impressively Picturesque "Summer Cottage," complete with dovecote tower (Figure 55).[52] Among the more lavish dwellings, Wheeler describes a "Gothic Suburban Villa" in detail, from plan to interior decoration to warming and ventilating (Figure 56). Despite the title he gives this mansion, the use of historical style here, as elsewhere in Wheeler's writings, takes second place to practical considerations.

Another member of this group, the "Large Villa in Roman Style"[53] (Figure 57) whose location is not given, is one that in plan and compositional type fits into a series of like Italianate houses ranging from that published in A. J. Downing's *Cottage Residences* of 1842 to Richard Upjohn's Edward King house of 1845–47 in Newport, Rhode Island, as published in Downing's *Architecture of Country*

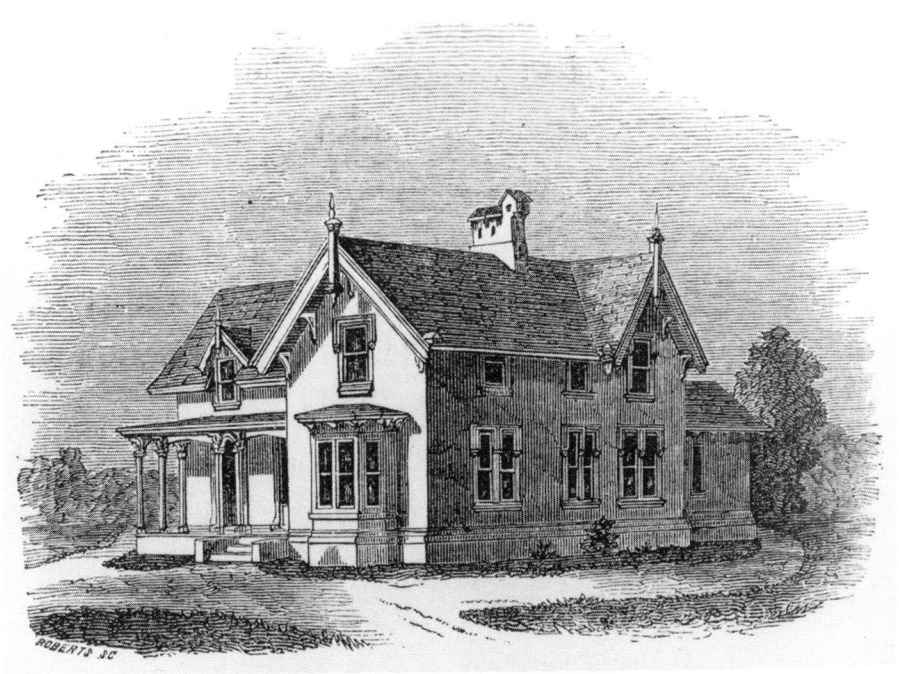

Figure 54. (top) *"Gothic Parsonage" for an Episcopal congregation in Massachusetts, ca. 1851–55. (From* Homes for the People.*)*

Figure 55. (bottom) *"Summer Cottage," ca. 1851–55. (From* Homes for the People.*)*

[93]

Figure 56.
"Gothic Suburban Villa," ca. 1851–55.
(From Homes for the People.*)*

Figure 57.
"Large Villa in Roman Style," ca. 1851–55.
(From Homes for the People.*)*

Houses of 1850; Henry Austin's Norton house in New Haven of 1849; the "Suburban Villa" Wheeler himself published in his *Rural Homes* of 1851; and the William Arnold house of 1854–56 in Bangor, Maine, probably by a local architect in possession of a useful library.[54] Such was the interaction of architects, buildings, and publications in the middle of the nineteenth century, and such was Wheeler's participation in that interaction.

Epilogue

After thirteen years in America, in the first days of 1860 Wheeler returned to England with his family for reasons about which we can only speculate: the unsettled political climate in advance of the Civil War, lack of recognition by his colleagues at the A.I.A., homesickness? He had had a rather successful career in the States, with two popular books and many executed buildings to his credit, yet something drove him to return. He continued his practice in England, billing himself as architect, surveyor, and civil engineer, with offices until 1869 at 16 Hawley Square, Margate. An entry in the 1868 *Architects, Engineers, and Building-Trades Directory* published in London summarized the range of his practice: "railway buildings, banks, churches, mansions, and private residences in the United States and England; [he] has also been engaged in laying out lands, and in sanitary appliances." The documented catalogue of his design work in America includes all of the above except railway stations. As odd as it seems, no Wheeler-designed buildings have to date been located in his native country.

Overlooked when architects formed the American Institute of Architects, Wheeler now found support for his candidacy in the Royal Institute of British Architects (R.I.B.A.). At this period in the nineteenth century, membership in the R.I.B.A. was limited to a small fraction of those in the profession, namely, gentleman architects.[1] Wheeler met the qualifications, for on 11 February 1867, recommended by Fellows George Godwin, editor of *The Builder*; William Slater, a former fellow apprentice of R. C. Carpenter; and H. A. Derbyshire, he became a member, at the full rank of Fellow.[2] He also, about this time, moved from Margate to Kilburn in London, where he would reside until 1873 when he presumably retired, for he was dropped then from the R.I.B.A. rolls for nonpayment of dues.

According to the late Jill Allibone, architectural historian in London, scant available information exists regarding Wheeler's career in England. He did, in February 1868, read two papers before an Ordinary General Meeting of the R.I.B.A.; both concerned the "Peculiarities of Domestic Architecture in America."[3] A summary of part of his address, namely the description of a "New York Up-Town House" was subsequently published in *The Builder*.[4]

That summary began by warning a visitor to America that he will not find "subjects of aesthetic value for his note book," although there are other things worthy of investigation. His comments reflect the tilt of his work in this country. He goes on to say that "there is nothing in public buildings . . . to show the dawn of a new development, and that in . . . domestic architecture must be sought the germ of a national style, if such a flower is ever to bloom on transatlantic soil!" One may study American domestic architecture, he said, and "learn a useful lesson, not without advantage in its application" in England. "American architectural art is in a transition state, but from its domestic buildings," he fully believed, "is the embodiment of some fixed principles of design to spring." Although Wheeler mentioned the influence in the United States of English, French, Italian, and German styles, his discussion here, as in his American books, was largely devoted to location, planning, structure, heating, ventilating, and other practical considerations. In much of this he pointed to differences between English and American domestic design, especially in urban dwellings. These, he wrote, are "not French, nor . . . English, although possessing features common to both countries; and if the newly-acquired wealth of the citizens leads to some vulgarity of display, I do not know that we can afford to say much in the way of censure in face of examples we can call to mind at home." The reading of the R.I.B.A. paper drew comments from Charles Barry, Thomas L. Donaldson, Robert Kerr, and J. B. Papworth, all of a practical nature.

By 1871 Wheeler had once again published a book on domestic architecture. Reviews of *The Choice of a Dwelling* in the literary journals were generally positive. The critic for *The Athenaeum* thought that "Mr. Wheeler offers the largest, most carefully prepared, and, on the whole, wisest and most comprehensive collection . . . of pieces of advice on the subject."[5] That for *The Illustrated Review*, while complaining of the "superfluity of volumes treating of the planning and building of an English gentleman's house," wrote that Wheeler's book "claims favourable notice." The most valuable section, he thought, was the author's "account of American house-planning," for most of what else appeared in the book seemed, in his opinion, hardly new.[6] *Choice* seems to have been popular, however, for a correspondent in *The Illustrated Review*, somewhat exaggeratedly no doubt, claimed that copies of the work were to be "met with even in houses of the humblest families."[7]

The new volume was far better received by the editors of *The Builder*, a professional review, than *Homes for the People* had been sixteen years earlier when they accused Wheeler of plagiarism. This may have been because he wrote in the preface that the work had been suggested by the distinguished London publisher John Murray. (This would have been the third of that name.) The review considered that Wheeler had neatly compounded his knowledge of British domestic architecture with the experience of his practice in America to produce an informative manual for general public and architect alike. "As we close the book, and turn from its alternate references to New and Old England, we feel it is a gain."[8] Perhaps this reviewer was too polite to mention that Wheeler had here again plagiarized, but only himself, by reprinting a number of designs from *Homes for the People*.

Until English architectural commissions are discovered, *The Choice of a Dwelling* must stand as Wheeler's final work in the profession. By 1874 he had moved out of London and established himself in Sussex County. With what must have been "a touch of nostalgia," in 1881 he named his home "Brooklyn." The last directory listing for Gervase Wheeler occurred in 1889, and in April 1890 probate of his will was granted to his widow, Catherine Brewer Wheeler.[9]

Gervase Wheeler came to America in 1847, perhaps with the hope of introducing and practicing newly formulated British precepts of ecclesiastical architecture. In the face of both peer and client resistance, however, and his difficult personality as displayed at Brunswick, he did not pursue this path, falling back instead, for the most part, on the practice of domestic design. In this he proved to be influential.

Unlike the majority of his American contemporaries, Wheeler was well versed early on in the philosophies of the Picturesque and Ruskinian "truth and fitness." It was this background that enabled him to take part in the development and interpretation of American domestic architecture, especially as it inclined toward a Picturesque point of view. His Boody House continues to attract attention. His design for the Olmstead House is to this day considered a primary example of romantic eclecticism in a timber Gothic mode. The Barry House ranks among the important surviving mid-century Italianate villas. Wheeler tended to design actual commissions for a socially upscale clientele, and, based on the evidence of documented work, such as the Boody and Barry Houses, Brookwood, the Insurance Company of North America, and the Williams Chapel, he typically designed the projects but did not supervise their construction.

Regardless of his several important executed commissions, it was the popular appeal and acceptance of Wheeler's published works that primarily formed his contribution to the domestic architecture of mid-nineteenth-century America. Through his publications, many of the ideals of the Picturesque, such as the relationship of house to site and Ruskin's and Downing's concept of fitness, reached a broad public audience. His work appealed at once to the country gentleman looking for a residence expressive of the new philosophies of the age, and the middle-class person seeking a comfortable cottage. With so many of his houses gone or, if existing, unidentified, it is to his books on rural architecture that one must go to assess his merits. Judging by the reviews those books received on publication, his American contemporaries, if not recent architectural history, placed his contribution to mid-nineteenth-century domestic design in this country on nearly a par with that of Downing.

Appendix
Wheeler's Addresses in the United States

The following office (o) and residential (r) addresses are taken from city directories, ads, and, where a month is noted, letterheads.

1847, Apr	29 Greenwich Street, New York City (o/r not specified)
1846-4	77 Federal Street, Brunswick, Maine (r)
1848-49	Unknown address in New Haven (r)
1849-50	Janes's Building, 216½ Main Street (o); American House (r), Hartford
1850, Dec	70 Walnut Street, Philadelphia (o/r not specified)
1851, Feb	University Building, Washington Square, New York (o)
1852, May–Nov	Hubbard's Building, Main Street, Norwich (o)
Ca. 1853	Europe and London
1853-54	55 Trinity Building, 111 Broadway, New York (o); 1 Elm Place, Brooklyn (through 1859: [r])
1855	Nassau Bank Building, 7 Beekman Street, New York (o)
1856-57	430 Broome Street, New York (o)
1858-59	18 Williams Street, New York (o)
1860	Listed at Post Office Building, Brooklyn (o) but departed for England early January

Notes

Introduction

1. Information about Wheeler's English years was supplied by the late Jill Allibone. See her entry on Wheeler in the *Macmillan Encyclopedia of Architects*, Adolf K. Placzek, ed., New York: The Free Press, 1982, 388–89. It should be noted, however, that much new information is now available. See Holmes à Court Family History, available on line at holmesacourt.org, and John Culme, *Directory of Gold and Silversmiths*, London: ACC, 1987, 478. According to Culme, Gervase *père*'s wife was named Mary, and the couple also had a daughter, Matilda, born in 1818. From an obituary notice in the *Gentleman's Magazine* 35 (January 1851) we learn of a second daughter, Ann-Eliza. In the same periodical for January 1841 there is an obituary of Gervase *père*, who died in November 1840.

2. He styles himself thus in the letter cited in note 4. The first edition of *Cockford's Clerical Directory*, 1858, calls him Sub-Dean of Her Majesty's Chapel Royal; Confessor to the Household; and Chaplain in Ordinary to the Queen, 1847.

3. Everard M. Upjohn, *Richard Upjohn: Architect and Churchman*, New York: Columbia University Press, 1939 (reprint, Da Capo Press, 1968), 82.

4. Wesley to Wheeler, 28 August 1848, Bowdoin College Library, George J. Mitchell Department of Special Collections and Archives, Chapel Papers (hereafter Chapel Papers). Since this letter is found at Bowdoin Wheeler may have waved it around to suggest his social standing among the clergy.

5. James F. O'Gorman, *Henry Austin: In Every Variety of Architectural Style*, Middletown, Conn.: Wesleyan University Press, 2008, Appendix C.

6. Hoppin to Woods, 8 March 1847, Chapel Papers.

7. Goldsmiths Company Apprentice Book II, 161. See also the *Architects' Engineers' and Building Trades' Directory*, London: Wyman, 1868, 143.

8. Phoebe Stanton, *Pugin*, London: Thames & Hudson, 1971; Paul Atterbury, *A. W. N. Pugin: Master of Gothic Revival*, New Haven, Conn.: Yale University Press, 1995; and Rosemary Hill, *God's Architect: Pugin and the Building of Romantic Britain*, London: Allan Lane, 2007.

9. Warshaw Collection of Business Americana, Archives Center, National Museum of American History, Smithsonian Institution, Box 3, Folder 20. We owe this extraordinary find to Jeffery Cohen.

10. Wheeler to Woods, 14 August 1847, Chapel Papers. The word "Catholic" is written with a grossly exaggerated capital "C," as if he intended to emphasize what he meant.

11. Stanton, *Pugin*, 179.

12. *Early Victorian Architecture in Britain*, New York: Da Capo Press, 1972, 115.

13. Hoppin to Woods, 4 August 1847, Chapel Papers.

14. Barrington Kaye, *The Development of the Architectural Profession in England*, London: George Allen & Unwin, 1960, 83.

15. Justin Wintle, ed., *Makers of Nineteenth Century Culture*, London: Routledge & Kegan Paul, 1982, 530–31.

16. *Harper's* 4 (1851), 137.

17. Christopher Hussey, *The Picturesque: Studies in a Point of View*, London: Frank Cass & Co., 1967, 209.

18. *Architecture: Nineteenth and Twentieth Centuries*, Baltimore: Penguin Books, 1971, 258.

19. *Early Victorian Architecture in Britain*, 427.

20. Hussey, *The Picturesque*, 212.

21. *Homes for the People*, 92.

22. *Rural Homes*, 245–55; *Encyclopaedia*, 595–619.

23. *Homes For the People*, 145.

24. *Bulletin of the American Art Union*, 1851, 28–29.

25. *Rural Homes*, 196.
26. *Homes for the People*, 211–12.
27. *Homes for the People*, 194.
28. *Homes for the People*, 133.
29. *Rural Homes*, 49 and 177; Luther Bell, *The Practical Methods of Ventilating Buildings*, Boston: Dickenson Printing Est., 1848. Wheeler actually footnotes the publication of Bell's "Address to the Massachusetts Medical Society," 1848.
30. *Rural Homes*, 145; [Susan Fenimore Cooper], *Rural Hours*, New York: George P. Putnam, 1850, 380–85.
31. Wheeler, 264; Frederika Bremer, *The Homes of the New World*, London: Arthur Hall Virtue & Co., 1853.
32. *Rural Homes*, 272–73. Wheeler spells the name Kaimes.
33. See for example, Kenneth Hafertepe, "An Inquiry into Thomas Jefferson's Ideas of Beauty," *Journal of the Society of Architectural Historians* 59 (June 2000), 216–31.
34. *Homes for the People*, 194. In particular he cited the April 1847 issue of *The Mechanics' Magazine*.
35. *Homes for the People*, 133, 194, 314, and 408; *Rural Homes*, 215.
36. See note 9.
37. *Rural Homes*, 28; see also 109 and 307.
38. For Wheeler as decorative designer in the latest polychrome fashion see Kathleen Curran, "The Romanesque Revival, Mural Painting, and Protestant Patronage in America," *The Art Bulletin* 81 (1999), 693–722, and her *The Romanesque Revival*, University Park: The Pennsylvania State University Press, 2003, 271–74.
39. *Homes for the People*, 6; see also 93.
40. A Gervase Wheeler is credited with English versions of lyrics written in these languages for publishers J. L. Peters and William Dressler in the late 1850s. Music by Donizetti, Hoffman, Scochopole and Kücken. Details available at the University of Michigan library on line. A Gervase Wheeler also wrote the lyrics to "The Song of the Ocean Telegraph," published by Dressler in 1858. See "History of the Atlantic Cable & Submarine Telegraphy" on line. We can find no other Gervase Wheeler in New York during these years.
41. *Rural Homes*, 281.

42. *Rural Homes*, 232; Patrick Barry, *The Fruit Garden*, Rochester: self-published, 1851.
43. See Elspeth Cowell, "Samuel Sloan, Pattern Books, and the Question of Professional Identity," in Kenneth Hafertepe and James F. O'Gorman, eds., *American Architects and Their Books, 1840–1915*, Amherst: University of Massachusetts Press, 2007, 95–128.
44. Daniel Harrison Jacques, *The House: A Pocket Manual of Rural Architecture*, New York: Fowler & Wells, 1859, 20, 27.
45. Constance M. Greiff, *John Notman Architect*, Philadelphia: The Athenaeum, 1979, 40.
46. Wheeler to Bowdoin College, "Design for Decoration of Side Walls of Bowdoin College Chapel," 6 April 1847, Chapel Papers.
47. Henry H. Saylor, *The A.I.A.'s First Hundred Years*, Washington: The Octagon, 1957, 4.
48. Saylor, *A.I.A.'s First Hundred Years*, 29.
49. Greiff, *John Notman Achitect*, 41–43.
50. Evarard Upjohn, *Richard Upjohn*, 134–56.
51. Saylor, *A.I.A.'s First Hundred Years*, 54. Diaries of Isaiah Rogers (Avery Architectural Library, Columbia University), February 1840.
52. See note 9.
53. Wheeler to Reverend Calvin Durfee, 14 July 1857. Williamsiana Collection, Williams College Archives.
54. Insurance Company of North America, Directors' Minutes, 1850, 90. (CIGNA Corporate Archives, Philadelphia).
55. Natalie B. E. Stewart, "George Ellwanger and Patrick Barry, Romantic Builders," MA thesis, University of Rochester, 1985, 60.
56. Bruce B. McElvein, "Williams College Architecture," Honors thesis, Williams College, 1979, 177–79.
57. *The Genessee Farmer* 13, (June 1852), 197.
58. Wheeler to Joseph McKeen, 12 December 1847, Chapel Papers.
59. Wheeler to Woods, 5 May 1848, Chapel Papers.
60. Wheeler to Woods, 12 May 1848, Chapel Papers.
61. Wheeler to Woods, 27 September 1848, Chapel Papers.
62. Wheeler to Woods, 23 November 1848, Chapel Papers.

63. Wheeler to Woods, 2 May 1848, Chapel Papers.
64. Wesley to Wheeler, 28 August 1848, Chapel Papers.
65. Holmes à Court Family History on line. Wheeler mentions "Mr. Hyde my wife's father" in a letter to Upjohn of 17 March 1851 (Upjohn Papers, Manuscripts and Archive Division, New York Public Library. Hereafter, Upjohn Papers).
66. Seven children are listed in the Holmes à Court Family History on line. A one-and-a-half-year-old son, Gervase Morris Wheeler, died at the family's Elm Place home in Brooklyn on 11 January 1857 (*New York Herald*, 12 January 1857, 5). In his *The Choice of a Dwelling* (191), published in England in 1871, Wheeler mentions looking through plans of American commissions. Perhaps these drawings will one day surface in the possession of one of his descendents.
67. Hoppin to Woods, 10 April 1847, Chapel Papers.
68. Hoppin to Woods, 4 August 1847, Chapel Papers.
69. Sidney Fisher Diaries, 12 December 1849, Manuscript Collection, Historical Society of Pennsylvania.
70. Statement by Woods, no date, Chapel Papers.
71. Wheeler to Woods, 20 February 1848, Chapel Papers.
72. Wheeler to Woods, no date (probably spring 1848), Chapel Papers.
73. Wheeler to Woods, no date (probably 1848), Chapel Papers.
74. Fisher Diaries, 12 December 1849.

New York City, 1847
1. Ancestry.com lists his date of birth as 1824. Age at death as 65 in 1889. New York Passenger Lists, 1820–1957, 1847: Microfilm roll: M237_65; line 4, list number 41; 1881 census available at Ancestry.com (listed erroneously as "Geroate Wheeler"); *New York Times*, 9 January 1860.
2. And maybe lyricist, if he was that Gervase Wheeler who wrote the lyrics to "The Song of the Ocean Telegraph," a popular air published by William Dressler in New York in 1858. See www.atlantic-cable.com/music. And see Introduction note 40.

3. Hoppin to Woods, 8 March 1847, George J. Mitchell Department of Special Collections and Archives, Bowdoin College Library, Chapel Papers.
4. Letterhead, 6 April 1847, Chapel Papers.
5. Hoppin to Woods, 4 May 1847, Chapel Papers.
6. *National Academy of Design Exhibition Record, 1826–1860*, New York: New York Historical Society, 1943, 195. The whereabouts of this drawing are unknown.
7. Wheeler to Woods, 14 August 1847, Chapel Papers.

Brunswick, Maine, 1847–1848
1. Curran, "The Romanesque Revival," and *The Romanesque Revival*, and Ernest Christian Helreich, *Religion at Bowdoin College*, Brunswick: Bowdoin College, 1981. See too William Pierson's unpublished paper, "Richard Upjohn, Leonard Woods, and the Bowdoin College Chapel Conspiracy," a copy of which is filed with the Chapel Papers. For Wheeler's stay in Brunswick in general see John Ward's unpublished papers, written in the 1980s, now on file at the Maine Historic Preservation Commission in Augusta.
2. Hoppin to Woods, 8 March 1847, Chapel Papers.
3. Woods to Hoppin, 31 July 1847, Chapel Papers.
4. Everard Upjohn, *Richard Upjohn*, New York: Columbia University Press, 1939 (reprint Da Capo Press, 1968).
5. See Introduction note 38.
6. Woods to Hoppin, 31 July 1847, Chapel Papers.
7. Hoppin to Woods, 4 August 1847, Chapel Papers.
8. Woods to Hoppin, 31 July 1847, Chapel Papers.
9. Hoppin to Woods, 4 August 1847, Chapel Papers.
10. At his death in 1878, Woods left furniture and money to "two esteemed friends, Caroline and Emeline Weld, of Brunswick." *New York Times*, 6 February 1879, 3.
11. Hoppin to Woods, 10 April 1847, Chapel Papers.

12. Wheeler to the Building Committee, 29 September 1847, Chapel Papers.

13. Wheeler to the Building Committee, 1 October 1847, Chapel Papers.

14. Wheeler to Upjohn, 26 October 1847, Upjohn Papers, Manuscripts and Archives Division, New York Public Library. (Hereafter Upjohn Papers.) Transcripts of relevant letters from this collection are available in Chapel Papers.

15. Wheeler to Woods, 23 January 1848, Chapel Papers.

16. It should be noted that Wheeler was not meant to execute the design himself. In his letter to Woods from New Haven of 27 September 1847 (Chapel Papers) he says he has found a man to do just that: Guiseppe Guidicini, "an educated gentleman and one who studied for and for a while practiced the profession of Architect in Europe." Guidicini did not work at Bowdoin but he did execute the decorations on the interior of Henry Austin's Morse house (Victoria Mansion) in Portland, Maine.

17. Wheeler to Upjohn, 26 October 1847, Upjohn Papers. It should be noted that this was not true fresco but "fresco secco"; that is, the paint was applied to dry surfaces.

18. Wheeler, "Description of Decoration of the Library," 15 December 1847, Chapel Papers.

19. Wheeler to Woods, 12 May 1848, Chapel Papers.

20. *Bulletin of the American Art Union*, 1851, 62. Thanks to Earle Shettleworth and Arlene Palmer Schwind for notice of this description.

21. John Ward, "Gervase Wheeler," 15. Unpublished paper, Maine Historical Preservation Commission.

22. Woods, undated statement, possibly the end of 1847, Chapel Papers.

23. Wheeler to Woods, 10 May 1848, Chapel Papers. Drawings for the house are also mentioned in Woods to Wheeler, 19 May [1848].

24. Denys Peter Myers, *Maine Catalog*, Portland: Maine State Museum, 1974, 118–19.

25. Deborah Thompson, ed., *Maine Forms of American Architecture*, Camden, Maine: Downeast Magazine, 1976, 164–66. The author of this section, William B. Miller, writes that the existing color is original. This may be true for the walls, but one doubts the white-painted trim.

26. *Appleton's Cyclopedia of American Biography*, 281.

27. *The Horticulturalist* 4 (August 1849), frontispiece and 77–79; A. J. Downing, *The Architecture of Country Houses*, 1850 (reprint New York: Dover Publications, 1969), Design XXV, 298–304; William H. Brown, *The Carpenter's Assistant*, revised by Lewis E. Joy, Boston: Edward Livermore, 1853, 42.

28. Daniel D. Reiff, *Houses from Books*, University Park: The Pennsylvania State University Press, 2000, 66–67.

29. *Architectural Period Houses Inc.*, Princeton, Massachusetts, 1978. Courtesy Earle Shettleworth. On the other hand, it has recently shown up online as an example of poor design: www.backroadhome.com/house-poor-plans.

30. *The Horticulturalist* 4 (August 1849), 77.

31. Earle Shettleworth, Director of the Maine Historic Preservation Commission, thinks that the John G. Richardson house in Bath, Maine, of about 1850, may have been based on a Wheeler design similar to the Boody House. There are unsigned drawings for the house at the Bowdoin College Library, but written notations are not in Wheeler's hand.

New Haven, Connecticut, 1847–49

1. See James F. O'Gorman, *Henry Austin*, Middletown, Conn.: Wesleyan University Press, 2008.

2. Wheeler to Woods, 27 September 1847, Chapel Papers.

3. An unidentified design for a small church or chapel in the Henry Austin Papers at Yale may or may not reflect this project. See O'Gorman, *Austin*, Appendix C.

4. Wheeler to Woods, 27 September 1847, Chapel Papers.

5. Franklin Bowditch Dexter, *Biographical Sketches of the Graduates of Yale College*, VI, New Haven, Conn.: Yale University Press, 1912, 607, a reference we owe to Peter Knapp.

6. Woods to Upjohn, 17 July 1851, Upjohn Papers.

7. Wesley to Wheeler, 28 August 1848, Chapel Papers.

8. Wheeler to Woods, 27 September 1848, Chapel Papers. Wheeler may have cast a

jaundiced eye on Austin's domestic work as well. In *Rural Homes* (282) he wrote that "any where within fifty miles of New Haven . . . you see houses, Gothic, Moorish(!), Italian, or Egyptian, with the same flat roofs that look like box-lids shut down." This could be a reference to the work of his recent associate. See O'Gorman, *Austin*, chapter 2.

9. O'Gorman, *Austin*, 139–40.

10. *The Home Journal*, 14 June 1851.

11. There is also a sheet of interior stair details.

12. James F. O'Gorman, ed., *Drawing Toward Home*, Boston: Historic New England, 2010.

13. But see O'Gorman, *Austin*, Appendix B.

Hartford, Connecticut, 1849

1. *Well's City Directory for Hartford*, 1849.

2. Wheeler to Upjohn, 18 June 1849, Upjohn Papers.

3. *The Horticulturalist* 3 (June 1849) 573; *The Literary World* 4 (April 1849), 337.

4. June 1849, 560–61; August 1849, 77–79. The latter reappeared in Downing's *Architecture of Country Houses* (see Fig. 5).

5. *The Horticulturalist* 4 (September 1849), 144.

6. *The Horticulturalist* 3 (June 1849), 560. It has already been suggested here that this might reflect Wheeler's project for the President's House at Bowdoin.

7. *Rural Homes*, 72–77. He also gives the owner's name as Olmsted.

8. Vincent J. Scully, Jr., *The Shingle Style and the Stick Style*, New Haven, Conn.: Yale University Press, 1955, li-lii.

9. Robert J. Guter, "The Willows at Fosterfields," Historic Structures Report, Morristown, New Jersey, 1983. The house may also have inspired a variant, the Hartwell Carver house in Pittsford, New York, of 1853. Thanks to Jean France for this information.

10. In *Rural Homes*, 34. Wheeler mentions a towered Italian villa erected on the Hudson from his design.

11. John Zukowsky, *Hudson River Houses: Edwin Whitefield's "The Hudson River and Railroad Illustrated,"* Croton-on-Hudson, N.Y.: North River Press, 1981, 50.

12. *The Horticulturalist* (November 1856), 497.

13. 6th edition, 1859, 552.

14. A. A. Turner, *Villas on the Hudson*, New York: Appleton, 1860).

15. *The Knickerbocker or New-York Monthly Magazine*, 1860, 137, 142.

16. Martha J. Lamb, *The Homes of America*, New York: D. Appleton & Co., 1879, 162, 224.

17. Turner, *Villas on the Hudson*; John Zukowsky, *Hudson River Villas*, New York: Rizzoli, 1985, 107.

18. Anna Wells Rutledge, *Cumulative Record of Exhibition Catalogues, . . . 1807–1870*, Philadelphia: American Philosophical Society, 1955, 251. He is listed as living at 70 Walnut Street.

19. Egbert W. Richards, *Two Centuries Under Covenant, A History of the Berlin Congregational Church, 1775–1975*, Berlin, Conn., 1975, 43.

Philadelphia, Pennsylvania, 1849–1850

1. Notices in the *Philadelphia Inquirer* (24 April 1850), *Trenton State Gazette* (29 April 1850), and *North American and United States Gazette* (4 April 1851) tell us that Lieutenant Harry Ingersoll, having lately come into possession of half a million, has left the Navy and intends to live in a style worthy of his means. He had purchased a beautiful property in Bristol Township "which he designs as a permanent home." This information presents something of a problem, for Ingersoll had already built a house, Medary, in North Philadelphia, in 1847–48, from the design of John Notman. According to Fisher's Diaries, 1 November 1847, Ingersoll consulted with Downing then, so the landscape architect must have been the connection between Ingersoll and Wheeler, but the latter, it seems, never produced a house for the former. See Constance M. Greiff, *John Notman Architect*, Philadelphia: The Athenaeum, 1979, 129–30.

2. Warshaw Collection of Business Americana, Archives Center, National Museum of American History, Architecture, Box 3, Folder 20.

3. Sidney George Fisher, "Diaries 1934 to 1871," 5 November and 12 December 1849. Historical Society of Pennsylvania.

4. Fisher, "Diaries," 23 December 1849.

5. Fisher, "Diaries," 16 August 1850, 16 June and 31 December 1851.

6. Downing (Sargent, ed.), *Theory and Practice of Landscape Gardening*, 555.

7. *Country Houses*, 330.

8. *Country Houses*, 330–38.

9. *Smedley's Atlas of the City of Philadelphia*, Philadelphia: J. B. Lippincott, 1862, 22nd ward, *Atlas of the City of Philadelphia*, Philadelphia: G. M. Hopkins, 1885, 22nd ward, and *Insurance Map of the City of Philadelphia*, Philadelphia: Ernest Hexamer & Son, 1898, 33.

10. Fisher, "Diaries," 12 December 1849.

11. *Journal of the Select Council*, Philadelphia: Cressy & Markley, 1850, 45.

12. *Journal of the Common Council*, Philadelphia: King & Baird, 1850, 170.

13. I.N.A., "Directors' Minutes," 26 February, 198; 12 March, 19; and 24 December 1850, 216.

14. Thomas H. Montgomery, *A History of the Insurance Company of North America*, Philadelphia: Press of Review Publishing & Printing Co., 1885, op. 90.

15. The ground floor front shown in the illustration may well be an alteration by Frank Furness, ca. 1870, according to Michael J. Lewis.

16. *Choice*, 132–35.

17. In *Rural Homes* (p. 161). Wheeler illustrates a "Small Cottage," "of pleasing and picturesque" appearance built from his designs in two places, without naming the places.

New York City, 1850–1851

1. The first of a series of Wheeler's articles for *The Home Journal*, was signed "GW," New York, February 1851.

2. For the city directory listing see Dennis Steadman Francis, *Architects in Practice in New York City, 1840-1900*, New York: The Committee for the Preservation of Architectural Records, 1979.

3. Wheeler to Upjohn, 17 March 1851, Upjohn Papers.

4. Frank Luther Mott, *A History of American Magazines*, Cambridge, Mass.: Harvard University Press, 1938, vol. 2, 350.

5. Mott, *American Magazines*, vol. 1, 511.

6. *Home Journal*, 1 March to 19 April 1851.

7. *Home Journal*, 12 May 1855.

8. Yet in his later *Homes for the People* (248) he could write that the plantation house he designed for the South "has nothing about its plan . . . that would render it unsuited to the North."

9. *Rural Homes*, chapter 8.

10. In addition to the reviews cited below see those in *The American Whig Review* 14 (December 1851), 544, and in *The Living Age* 31 (6 December1851), 473 (quoting the *New York Courier*) and 32 (3 January 1852), 48 (quoting the *New York Evening Post*).

11. *Debow's* 12 (January 1852), 116.

12. *The Genessee Farmer* 13 (January 1852), 89.

13. *The American Whig Review* 14 (December 1851), 544.

14. *Genessee Farmer* 13 (January 1852), 16.

15. *Genessee Farmer* 13 (August 1852), 260.

16. *Sartain's Magazine* (1852), 102.

17. *The Horticulturist* 6 (December 1851), 567.

18. Francis R. Kowsky, *Country, Park, & City: The Architecture and Life of Calvert Vaux*, New York: Oxford University Press, 1998, 22–23.

19. *Literary World* 7 (July-December 1850), 91.

20. Abbott L. Cummings, "Asher Benjamin," *The Macmillan Encyclopedia of Architects* I, Adolf Placzek, ed., New York: The Free Press, 1982, 178.

21. *The Literary World* 9 (November 1851), 388.

22. Don Seitz, "Best Sellers of the Fifties," *The Publishers' Weekly* 28 (28 January 1922), 183–84.

23. *North American Miscellany and Dollar Review* (1851), 164.

24. *Genessee Farmer* 13 (February 1852), 47–50.

25. *Home Journal*, 8 November 1851.

Norwichtown, Connecticut, 1851–1852

1. Upjohn to Woods, 15 July 1851, Chapel Papers.

2. Woods to Upjohn, 17 July 1851, Chapel Papers.

3. *Norwich Weekly Courier* (12 May to 3 November 1852), 1; *Genessee Farmer* 13 (June 1852), 197.

4. 54: described as a house of 50-foot front built of brick and stone.

5. *The Horticulturalist* n.s. 3 (August 1853), 373; *Homes for the People*, 155–74; *Choice of a Dwelling*, 168.

6. Thanks to Christopher Wigren for this information. The original street number was 45.

7. Benjamin Tinkham Marshall, *A Modern History of New London*, New York: Lewis Historical Publishing Co., 1922, II, 578. Thanks to Dale Plummer, City Historian, and Christopher Wigren for this information. The place was later owned by F. A. Roath who named it Pinehurst.

8. *Homes for the People*, 218–31. Plan modified and republished in *Choice*, 191–93: "erected on a beautiful site on the slope of the Berkshire hills."

9. *Homes for the People*, 283–92.

New York City, 1853–1860

1. *Homes for the People*, 307.
2. *The Horticulturist* n.s. 3 (August 1853), 325.
3. (August 1853), 393, and (November 1853), 537.
4. *American Architect and Building News* 15 (February 1884), 75–76 (photo and caption); Michael Tomlan, Introduction to Henry Hudson Holly, *Country Seats and Modern Dwellings*, Watkins Glenn, N.Y.: Library of Victorian Culture, 1977; and George B. Tatum, Introduction to *Holly's Picturesque Country Seats*, New York: Dover, 1993. Compare, for just one example, design number 1, p. 33, in *Country Seats* with the stone house, p. 384, and small villa, pp. 85 and 88, in *Homes for the People*.
5. Holly, *Country Seats*, 31.
6. *Harper's* 53 (June 1876), 49, 217, 354.
7. Holly, *Country Seats*, Introduction.
8. *The Horticulturalist* n.s. 4 (May 1854), 230; Wheeler, *Homes for the People*, preface.
9. *The Horticulturalist* n.s. 3 (August 1853, frontispiece; Wheeler, *Homes for the People*, frontispiece; Wheeler, *Choice*, 186.
10. *The Horticulturist* n. s. 5 (1855), frontispiece; Wheeler, *Homes for the People*, 228.
11. *The Horticulturalist* n. s. 5 (1855), 294.
12. *Harper's Monthly Magazine* (July 1855), 261.
13. *The Knickerbocker or New York Monthly Magazine* (July 1855), 79.
14. *Transcript*, 8 May 1855, 1.
15. *The Builder*, 4 August 1855, 379.
16. N.s. 5 (1855), frontispiece.
17. *The Choice of a Dwelling*, London: John Murray, 1871, 139–42.
18. Congregational Churches in the United States, *A Book of Plans for Churches and Parsonages*, New York: Burgess & Co., 1853. See Gwen W. Steege, "The *Book of Plans* and the Early Romanesque Revival in the United States: a Study in Architectural Patronage," *Journal of the Society of Architectural Historians* 46 (September 1987), 215–27.
19. Plates from the *Book of Plans* were reprinted by George E. Woodward under the title *Rural Church Architecture* (Henry-Russell Hitchcock, *American Architectural Books*, New York: Da Capo Press, 1976, 1416–1417, dated between 1868 and 1875).
20. *Rural Homes*, 282.
21. *Homes for the People*, 50 (A Small Villa) and 348 (A Rustic Parsonage).
22. *Southern Tier Times* (Owego), 20 June, 5 April, and 10 May 1854; *Owego Gazette*, 20 June 1854, references owed to Gary Murray. The church is now called the First Presbyterian Union Church. See also online OwegoFPUC.org.
23. Architect-"signed" buildings in this period are uncommon in the United States and in England.
24. Alexander Cameron MacKenzie, *Retracing Old Paths; or, An Historical Sketch of the First Presbyterian Church and Society of Owego, N.Y.*, 1895, 47, 52–53.
25. In brief: the organ has been moved from the gallery above the entrance to an added recess beyond the reading desk, both towers have lost their terminals, and the building to the south of the church proper is later. It might be assumed that the white paint presently covering the brick exterior is a later, perhaps a Colonial Revival, alteration. There is evidence that the interior was once, perhaps originally, stenciled in bright colors as was common at this period. See O'Gorman, *Austin*, 95–97.
26. O'Gorman, *Austin*, 111–16.
27. Brice B. McElvein, "Williams College Architecture, 1790–1860," Honors Thesis, Williams College, 1979, 195. Documents in the

Williamsiana Collection, Williams College and on-line.

28. Wheeler to Durfee, 22 July 1857.

29. Whitney S. Stoddard, *Reflections on the Architecture of Williams College*, Williamstown, Mass.: Williams College, 2001, 46–47.

30. *Bankers' Magazine*, 761–68, a reference owed to Arthur Downs.

31. Mott, 2: 93–94.

32. In the same issue of the *Bankers' Magazine* appears a cut of the Italianate Seaman's Bank for Savings in New York City. Although not part of Wheeler's article, it could easily have been.

33. Unprocessed in PR 13 CN 1999:105, Prints and Drawings Division, Herbert Mitchell Architectural Drawings Collection. Bound into an Ellis & Slote blank book are plans of the basement, first and second floors, and four elevations in ink, watercolor, and graphite on linen. They are heavily foxed. My thanks to C. Ford Peatross for information and scans.

34. *Appleton's Cyclopaedia of American Biography* 1:181.

35. Ellwanger and Barry Daybook, No. 167, 29 January 1858, cited from Natalie B. E. Stewart, "George Ellwanger and Patrick Stewart, Romantic Builders," MA thesis, University of Rochester, 1985, 60. The house is recorded in the Historic American Buildings Survey. The ledger entry for payment to Wheeler includes $70 for George Ellwanger. Although there is no explanation for this payment, it may indicate that Wheeler also produced a design for an Ellwanger house.

36. According to the Historic American Buildings Survey, drawings existed as late as 1962 but then disappeared.

37. Stewart, 75. For Merwin Austin and A. J. Warner see O'Gorman, *Austin*, Appendix C.

38. *Rural Homes*, 28.

39. Warshaw Collection of Business Americana, Archives Center, National Museum of American History, Architecture, Box 3.

40. *Homes for the People*, 248–60.

41. Wheeler to Durfee, 14 July 1857, Williamsiana Collection, Williams College.

42. Warshaw Collection. While it is unsigned, the writing seems to be in his hand, and it is filed near Wheeler's project for the Farwell house previously discussed, but does not show the same plan. It has not been possible to obtain a publishable reproduction.

43. *Well's City Directory for Hartford*, 1849, 138.

44. Warshaw Collection, Architecture, Box 3, Folder 20.

45. *Courier*, May 12 to November 3, 1852, 1; *Farmer* 13 (June 1852), 197.

46. Sherman W. Adams, "The Hartford Park System," *Connecticut Magazine* 1 (1895), 174; John Alexopoulos, *The Nineteenth Century Parks of Hartford*, Hartford, Conn.: Hartford Architectural Conservancy, 1983, 16; Rudy J. Favretti, *Jacob Weidemann, Pioneer Landscape Architect*, Middletown, Conn.: Wesleyan University Press, 2007, 26–28.

47. In 1859 Wheeler received a commission to enlarge and improve the chancel of the Church of the Holy Trinity in Brooklyn, a building designed by Minard Lafever in 1844. The work primarily involved alterations to the reading desk and the addition of pews "in accordance with the original plan of the church." Landy, *Lafever*, 270. This is the architect's last known commission in America.

48. *Choice*, 141–44, with two plans. This is preceded by a discussion of New York town houses design by Charles Duggin, another immigrant English architect, 137–41.

49. *Homes for the People*, 258–59.

50. *Homes for the People*, 94–106.

51. *Homes for the People*, 327–31.

52. *Homes for the People*, 271–81; republished in *Choice*, 208.

53. *Homes for the People*, 145–55.

54. See Deborah Thompson, *Bangor, Maine 1769–1914: An Architectural History*, Orono: University of Maine Press: 1988, 281–84. One could of course add other examples to the sequence.

Epilogue

1. Spiro Kostof, *The Architect: Chapters in the History of a Profession*, New York: Oxford University Press, 1977, 194.

2. Nomination Papers, 1867, 36, R.I.B.A. Library. See Michael Tomlan's introduction to Henry Hudson Holly, *Country Seats & Modern Dwellings*, Walkins Glen, N.Y.: Library of Victorian Culture, 1977, note 5.

3. Sessional Papers of the Royal Institute of British Architects, London, 1868, 117–28 and 168–87.

4. *The Builder*, 11 April 1868, 262–63. This is not the house illustrated here as Fig. 33.

5. *The Athenaeum*, 20 April 1872, 502.

6. *The Illustrated Review*, May 1972, 661.

7. *The Illustrated Review*, January 1873, 23.

8. *The Builder*, 23 December 1871, 998.

9. Information from the late Jill Allibone. "A touch of nostalgia" was her phrase.

Index

Page numbers in *italics* indicate illustrations

American Institute of Architects (A.I.A.), 10–11, 12
Apology for the Revival of Christian Architecture in England, An (Pugin), 3
"Architectonics" (Long), 6
Architecture of Country Houses, The (Downing), 9, 24, 44–45, 56–57
Austin, Henry, 17, 29–33, 42, 69, 81
Austin, Merwin, 83

Barry, Charles, 31, 97
Barry, Patrick, 8, 83
Barry, Patrick, house, 11, 12, 82–84, *82*, *84*
Bartlett, Edwin, house ("Rockwood"), 39–42, *40*
Bell, Luther, 6
Berlin, Connecticut: Congregational Church, *41*, 42
Billings, Hammatt, 81
Blondel, Jean-François, 5–6
Boody, Henry Hill, 24
Boody, Henry Hill house, *Frontispiece*, 24–28, *25–27*, 35, 37, 44
Book of Plans for Churches and Parsonages, A, 66, 69–71, 73
Bowdoin College, Brunswick, Maine: Chapel Building, library decoration, 14, 18–23, *21*, president's house project, 11, 23–24
Bremer, Fredrika, 6
Brown, William, 28
Builder, The, 7, 67, 96–97
Bulfinch, Charles, 73
Bushnell, Horace, 87–88
Bushnell Park project, Hartford, Connecticut, 87–88
Butman, Benjamin, house, Worcester, Massachusetts, 28

Cabot and Chandler, 46
Carpenter, Richard Cromwell, 2–4, 16, 20, 29–30, *41*, 42, 73, 96
Carpenter's Assistant, The (Brown), 28

Carver, Hartwell, house, Pittsford, New York, 105n9
Christ Episcopal Church, Norwich, Connecticut, 58
Choice of a Dwelling, The (Wheeler), 48, 97–98
Cleaveland, Henry, 69
Columbian Drawing Book, The (Kuchel), 34, 50
Congregational Church project, 69–71
Cooper, Susan Fennimore, 6
Country bank projects, 77–81, *80*
Country Seats (Holly), 65–66
Cours d'Architecture (Blondel), 5

Davis, Alexander Jackson, 5, 9, 35, 49
Derbyshire, H. A., 96
Donaldson, Thomas L., 97
Downing, Andrew Jackson, 4–5, 6, 8, 24, 35, 39, 43–44, 54, 55–57, 69, 98
Duggin, Charles, 65
Durfee, Calvin, 75

Elements of Criticism (Kames), 6–7
Emerson, Ralph Waldo, 8
Encyclopaedia of Architecture (Gwilt), 5
Evangeline (Longfellow), 54

Farwell, O., house project, 85–86, *85*, *86*
First Presbyterian Church, Owego, New York, 71–73, *72*, *74–75*
Fisher, Henry C., house ("Brookwood"), 14, 43–45, *44*
Fisher Sidney, 14, 43
Fruit Garden, The (Barry), 8

Gerard, Benjamin, 43, 45
Godwin, George, 96
Goodwin, Francis, 5
Guidicini, Giuseppe, 104n16
Gwilt, Joseph, 5

Hartford, Connecticut: college chapel project, 29
Haviland, John, 45
Hitchcock, Henry-Russell, 3, 5

[111]

Holly, Henry Hudson, 65–66
Holly's Country Seats, 65–66
Holy Trinity Church, Brooklyn, New York, 108n47
Home, Henry (Lord Kames), 6–7
Home Journal, The, articles (Wheeler), 50–52
Homes for the People (Wheeler), 1, 5, 50, 64, 65–69, 71
Homes of the New World, The (Bremer), 6
Hopkins, Mark, 75
Hoppin, William J., 2, 3, 14, 16, 18–20
Horticulturist, The, 9, 24, 35, 39, 50, 65, 67, 69, 83
Hunt, Richard Morris, 11
Hussey, Christopher, 5

Ingersoll, Harry, 43, 105n1
Insurance Company of North America, Philadelphia, 11, 46–48, *47*
Italian Villa project, 32–33, *32*

Jane Eyre, 14
Jones, Owen, 5

Kames, Lord. *See* Home, Henry
Kerr, Robert, 97
Knight, Richard Payne, 4

Lafever, Minard, 81
Latrobe, Benjamin Henry, 10
Lebrun, Napoleon, 45
Long, Robert Cary, 6
Longfellow, Henry Wadsworth, 54
Loudon, John Claudius, 4, 8

Milizia, Francesco, 6
Modern Dwellings (Holly), 66
Modern Painters (Ruskin), 4
Morris, George, 50
Murray, John, 97

New Haven House Hotel, 31–32, *31*
New York townhouse, 69, *70*
Notman, John, 9, 10, 11, 81

Olmstead, Henry, house, 37–39, *37–38*
"On Perfecting a Home" (Wheeler), 50–51
Owego, New York: First Presbyterian Church, 71–73, *73*, 74–75

Papworth, J. B., 97
"Peculiarities of Domestic Architecture in America," (Wheeler), 96
Perkins, Joshua Newton, 59
Perkins, Joshua Newton, house, 59, *60–61*
Philadelphia, project for a County Court Building, 45–46
Philadelphia townhouse, 48, *48*
President's House, Bowdoin College, 11
Price, Uvedale, 4
Pugin, Augustus W. N., 2–4, 16, 20, 30

Renwick, James Jr., 69
Repton, Humphrey, 4
Revere, Joseph Warren, house ("The Willows"), Morristown, N.J, *38*, 39
Richardson, John G., house, Bath, Maine, 104n31
Rogers, Isaiah, 11
Royal Institute of British Architects (R.I.B.A.), 4, 96
Rural Architecture (Goodwin), 5
Rural Architecture (White), 5
Rural Homes (Wheeler), 5, 52–57
Rural Hours (Cooper), 6
Ruskin, John, 4, 6

St. Mary Magdalen, London, 3
St. Stephen's, Selly Park, Birmingham, 3
Sargent, Henry, 39
Seven Lamps of Architecture, The (Ruskin), 4
Slater, William, 96
Sloan, Samuel, 9
Stones of Venice, The (Ruskin), 4

Tatlock, Professor, and landscape project in Williamstown, Massachusetts, 87
Theory and Practice of Landscape Gardening, The (Downing), 39, 43
Travelers Club House, London, 31
True Principles of Pointed or Christian Architecture, The (Pugin), 3

Upjohn, Richard, 1–2, 10, 11, 12, 16–17, 18–22, 30, 34, 49–50, 58, 69, 75, 76

Vaux, Calvert, 10, 56
Vite de'più celebri architetti, Le (Milizia), 6

Walter, Thomas U., 10, 45
Warner, Andrew Jackson, 83
Weidenmann, Jacob, 88
Wesley, Sir Charles, 1–2, 13, 30
Wheeler, Catherine ("Kate") Brewer Hyde (wife), 13, 17
Wheeler, Gervase: advertising flyer, 2, 4, 7, 11–12, 85–86, *85*; on American domestic architecture, 6, 96–97; and the American Institute of Architects, 10, 12, 66, 96; arrival in the United States, 2, 8, 16, 98; client relations, 30, 58; criticized by Downing, 55–57; and decorative art, 2, 3, 5, 16–17, 18–24, 72–73; designs for church needlework, 3; drawings, 24, *25–26*, *32*, 34, 76, 81, 85–86, 103n66, 104n23; in England, 1–6, 96–98; and English Ecclesiology, 2, 3, 4, 29–30; European travel, 7–8, 65; health, 12–13; and Henry Hudson Holly, 65–66; life dates, 16; literary sources, 4–7, 8; as lyricist, 102n40, 103n2; professional fees, 11–12, 24; as landscape designer, 87; marriage and family, 13, 96, 98, 103nn65–66; personal characteristics, 13–15, 22; and the Picturesque, 4–5, 9, 28; as plagiarist, 7, 67, 97–98; and professionalism, 4, 10, 67, 98; public buildings, designer of, 32; religious affiliation, 1; relations with Upjohn, 18–22, 30, 34, 49–50, 58; reviews of publications, 4, 9–10, 35, 52, 54–57, 67–69, 97; and the Royal Institute of British Architects, 10, 96; and Ruskin, 4, 6; training in England, 2–4; as translator, 7–8

Wheeler, Gervase (father), 1–2, 101n1
White, John, 5
Williams College, Williamstown, Massachusetts: chapel (Goodrich Hall), 11, 12, 73–77, *76*, *78–79*
Willis, Nathaniel Parker, 50
Withers, Frederick C., 10
Woods, Leonard, Jr., 2, 13, 14, 18–24, 29–30, 58–59, 75

Garnet Books

Gervase Wheeler:
A British Architect in America
by Renée Tribert and James F. O'Gorman

Food for the Dead:
On the Trail of New England's Vampires
by Michael E. Bell

Early Connecticut Silver, 1700–1840
by Peter Bohan and Philip Hammerslough
Introduction and Notes by Erin Eisenbarth

The Connecticut River:
A Photographic Journey through
the Heart of New England
by Al Braden

Connecticut's Fife & Drum Tradition
by James Clark

The Old Leather Man:
Historical Accounts of a Connecticut
and New York Legend
by Daniel DeLuca

Post Roads & Iron Horses:
Transportation in Connecticut from
Colonial Times to the Age of Steam
by Richard DeLuca

Dr. Mel's Connecticut Climate Book
by Dr. Mel Goldstein

Westover School:
Giving Girls a Place of Their Own
by Laurie Lisle

Crowbar Governor:
The Life and Times of Morgan Gardner Bulkeley
by Kevin Murphy

Water for Hartford:
The Story of the Hartford Water Works
and the Metropolitan District Commission
by Kevin Murphy

Henry Austin:
In Every Variety of Architectural Style
by James F. O'Gorman

Making Freedom:
The Extraordinary Life of Venture Smith
by Chandler B. Saint and George Krimsky

Welcome to Wesleyan:
Campus Buildings
by Leslie Starr

Connecticut in the American Civil War:
Slavery, Sacrifice, Survival
by Matthew Warshauer

Stories in Stone:
How Geology Influenced
Connecticut History and Culture
by Jelle Zeilinga de Boer

ABOUT THE AUTHORS

Renée E. Tribert holds an MS in Preservation from the University of Pennsylvania. Formerly employed at the Stowe-Day Foundation and the New Britain Museum of American Art, she is currently associated with an environmental consulting firm and has served on the board of the Simsbury, Connecticut, Historical Society.

James F. O'Gorman is Professor Emeritus at Wellesley College and author of many works on the history of American architecture including *Henry Austin: In Every Variety of Architectural Style* (2008), also published by Wesleyan University Press. It won the annual Book Prize of Historic New England for 2009, and the Henry-Russell Hitchcock Award of the Victorian Society in America for 2010.

ABOUT THE DRIFTLESS CONNECTICUT SERIES

The Driftless Connecticut Series is a publication award program established in 2010 to recognize excellent books with a Connecticut focus or written by a Connecticut author. To be eligible, the book must have a Connecticut topic or setting or an author must have been born in Connecticut or have been a legal resident of Connecticut for at least three years.

The Driftless Connecticut Series is funded by the Beatrice Fox Auerbach Foundation Fund at the Hartford Foundation for Public Giving. For more information and a complete list of books in the Driftless Connecticut Series, please visit us online at http://www.wesleyan.edu/wespress/driftless.